10 STEPS

to

THE TOP

10 STEPS
—*to*—
THE TOP

MARIE JENNINGS

BCA
LONDON · NEW YORK · SYDNEY · TORONTO

This edition published 1992 by
BCA by arrangement with
Judy Piatkus (Publishers) Ltd of
5 Windmill Street, London W1

CN 5818

Printed in Great Britain

CONTENTS

ACKNOWLEDGEMENTS

In researching and writing this book, I have been helped by many organisations and by many distinguished people who have made it 'to the top'. It would be quite wrong not to acknowledge this help. It is because of it that the book should be of practical help to the reader.

My grateful thanks, therefore, to:

Senator Antonio Inoki of Japan
Jan Walsh
Professor Meredith Thring
John Patterson
Dr Elizabeth Nelson
Lady Wilcox
Jilly Cooper
Roderick Dewe
Barbara Barkovitch
Martin Smith
Dr Alexander King
The Baroness Phillips of Fulham
David Wickes
Tom Douglas
Janet Brady
Vincent Duggleby
Dr Oonagh McDonald
The Baroness Platt of Writtle
Brian Locke
James Haswell
Jeff Meyers
Karen Pheasant
Martina Platz
Phil Kirkham
Harvey Thomas
David Pebber
John Pinnegar
Sir Denys Henderson

Thanks are also due to:

National Westminster Bank
British Telecom
British American Tobacco
ICI
Taylor Nelson
Hayashibara

Finally, my thanks also to my invaluable PA, Sue Williams, and my cheerful and industrious editor, Carol Franklin.

Quite simply, without their help this book could not have been written.

Marie Jennings
Bisley,
Stroud

PART ONE

▲

Introduction

First, a word of thanks. Thank you for your interest in the subject of this book. I believe that there is an enormous amount of urge, initiative and value in people that is waiting to be developed – not by government plans, but by people developing themselves through realising their potential, and for their own, personal satisfaction.

The book is intended as a practical guide, setting out in simple and concise terms how you, the reader, can plan your personal development. It starts by helping you to conduct a self-assessment, and to write your own script for successful development. Hopefully this will lead, in turn, to a happy and rewarding life.

Naturally, as the author, I wouldn't presume to draw only on my own experience and to exhort you to do as I did. Rather, I am going to try to distil that experience and use it in the book. In addition, I shall call on the experience of many people, and big and small organisations, with the authority and credentials to be of practical benefit to you, the reader. With their help, the book has become what I hope you will find is a valuable tool, enabling you to make more of your business and personal life. I hope it will also give you an insight into the factors which govern the decisions made about whom to promote in an organisation, and whose views will carry weight in the wider world.

The book contains many contributions, from those who have achieved much, and who have reached the top. What they have said about who they are, what they tried to do, what they achieved, and their views on what is important, provides a unique distillation from the 'university of life'.

What I have also tried to do is to make the book an easy read.

It is a firm belief of mine that time is the most precious asset of all. It should not, or need not, be wasted. It cannot be repeated. That one life we all enjoy must be rewarding – in the terms we, as individuals, believe to be important. For this reason we must all be that much more sensitive to ourselves, to know ourselves as we really are and what we want from life – especially (though by no means only) that part of our life spent at work.

There are, too, many different types of 'tops' or mountains to be climbed ... Not all of us want to become chief executive of a multi-national company and, while most of us could do with more money, not all of us are prepared to make the sacrifices that may be necessary to 'climb the greasy pole' to become a billionaire! For most of us, a happy satisfying life means having many and varied interests – and the money to give us the freedom to enjoy them. That, at least, is and has always been, my aim, my own special and private 'top', my personal mountain.

This, then, is the practical way forward – to achieve the potential in each and every one of us.

Looking Ahead in the World of Today and Tomorrow

To be of practical use, this book must give you a short glimpse of what the world may be like in the year 2000 and beyond. Then you can plan ahead.

In a thumbnail sketch this isn't easy.

First, it is important to take a look at how the world of work is changing. Business used to be seen as being like a pyramid, or as a series of mountains. But already significant changes are visible. Charles Handy has suggested that we are going to see more of the 'shamrock' organisation in which a small core of people work at the centre, striving to reach the top. Their needs are serviced by many more who are achieving fulfilment through meeting the individual standards and criteria they have set for themselves, and with the independence that comes of being an expert or a consultant, or an 'outworker' working from home. Those working in the different areas supporting the organisation, for example in research and development, in marketing and promotion, in counselling in all its different components, form the 'leaves' of the shamrock. In this new world of work, too, there will be more again who may be working part-time, in the recognition that their own list of priorities calls for more leisure-time to pursue their special interests.

It is important to recognise, too, the march of technology. To give some examples, today's world of work is already accepting the introduction of voice recognition techniques, adapted to computers; the use of biometrics (fingerprint signatures) for verification – to name only two. Progress will radically change the world of work, even as we know it today.

The different types of 'success' also need to be recognised. Some main types of success will be identified later in this book. You need to recognise and identify what spells 'success' for you.

Other changes also need to be taken on board. For example, it is likely that we will need to understand and use a lot more technology. This will make information and knowledge much more accessible to us. It will, however, mean that our lives will need to be adjusted, too. It is likely that we will be travelling less to remote offices or to the big cities. We will probably be using our homes more as our workplaces and making use of the telephone, TV screen or fax machine more as a point of access for many areas, including shopping as well as work. Even sitting in a jumbo jet miles above the earth we will be able to use the plane's telephones to order the machines in our home to do the chores, such as drawing the curtains, switching on the cooker and the lights, inspecting the guy who calls at the door to mend the washing machine, letting him in the house and then interrogating the washing machine to check that it is working properly when he has finished – and letting him go out again, while refusing non-scheduled callers!

Alas, there will be other changes, too. It is probable that the 'haves' will have more and the 'have nots' will have less. It will, therefore, be more important for those who can cope, to cope, and to ensure that some spare time and effort and, yes, money too, is available to help those who are less fortunate.

The Implications of Time

Time will still be our most precious commodity – but then it already is, although that realisation isn't too familiar or accepted yet. By the year 2000 it will be very self-evident. For most people, time is just something that passes. But for you, it probably has to be planned carefully – there is never enough of it. So you need to decide your priorities.

The changes with regard to time will have deeper implications for us all. For most people there will be more leisure-time available to be filled. How? Perhaps the working week will get shorter? Will this mean that we have to achieve as much, as regards work, in less time? What are the strains which such changes will make on family life, and on the social fabric of the nation? On the equilibrium of the world? This isn't easy to specify but, for example, we will need to plan more to ensure there is time for work, for the priorities of home and family, and for identifying and working at leisure interests which could range from hobbies to the fulfilment of continuing education in your chosen and favourite areas. And, indeed, for many of us there is always need to find time 'to stop and stare', to watch the grass grow.

At this time, too, we may – and should – be getting increasingly involved in community activities and could have 'adopted' a favourite good cause in another part of the world. All these factors will play a part in enabling us to lead a happy, satisfied and rewarding life in the fullest sense. You need to 'know yourself' to decide the right mix of components for you as an individual.

While the nature of work may be changed and changing, the mountains that remain to be climbed by the individual will be more exciting, more challenging and visible in fields which still lie hidden from us.

Economic and Other Factors

As far as the economic situation is concerned, things may be very different in this area too. Mostly this will be as a result of the international climate of opinion, and the pressures of many urgent issues. To name a few of these: Third World debt; the 'greenhouse' effect; the population explosion; the migration of peoples; the march of technology. But some factors may be working better for us than for our cousins in continental Europe. For example, it is thought that in the middle 1990s inflation in Britain may get down to, and stay at, some figure as low as 3 or 4 per cent. Also in Britain we should already have made – and paid for – the change from centrally managed to personal pensions. As a result the older generations should be better off. This, in turn, should release 'government' money in central budgets which may be put to other useful purposes. These purposes could include additional resources for health, for education, for community care. In addition, the major costs of many macro projects such as the Channel Tunnel, should have been met. As a result there should be more money in the private capital markets to underwrite worthwhile technological and other innovation – which should make life easier and more satisfying for us all.

These, then, are just a few factors which you should bear in mind when selecting the particular mountain you wish to climb to lead a happy, satisfying and rewarding life, in all senses of those words. Playing your part – as far as possible – in helping to ensure that the correct checks and balances are in place should lead to positive consequences in a (hopefully) more equitable society.

The Different Types of 'Top'

There are many different types of 'top', different sorts of mountains. It is desirable to identify them, and for you to recognise which one is for you. Remember, too that your own attitudes and goals may well evolve with time and experience.

Here are three of the more obvious examples.

The business mountain

Until, say, ten years ago there was a traditional route to the top in business. Organisations were structured, in the main, like pyramids. There were all those men and women at the bottom supporting the 'burden' of whole management structures. As one climbed the dizzy heights, there were fewer and fewer people at your level, with only a handful 'at the top'. The top represented power, influence, control – and, of course, money.

Things today are changing, fast. In the current enlightened management fashion, companies see the need to develop people as people – as I will illustrate in later chapters of this book. So, as the structure and nature of business changes, the potential it offers for a personally rewarding life – in terms of achievement, intellectual excitement, team and other leadership opportunities

– is better identified to attract those who may be interested in a business career which is evolving all the time.

The pyramid structure of business is less popular today; tomorrow it may be rare. In time, and as the wheel turns, it may come back into favour again. Meanwhile the development of individuals in business, helping them to achieve their potential, is increasingly being recognised, and given the resources it warrants by enlightened organisations.

The arts, sciences, academia

The march of new technology offers much to those who wish to climb these mountains. Whereas in the past the office environment meant that those who 'worked at home' or in other non-office environments were disadvantaged, things are changing. Today's proliferation of machines such as the ubiquitous word processor, the fax, conference calls and Telecom Gold, the answerphone etc., all bring a range of efficiency aids to the artist, the scientist, the academic – and to those in industry and commerce too – which means that his or her work can be much more efficient and effective – also, above all, cost-effective. The next generation will see the emergence of further new technologies, too.

To recognise this point, just look back to the days when (not so long ago) the zip fastener, velcro, staples, photocopiers, cameras and calculators, for example, were unreliable, rare or expensive as compared with those versions available to us today. How did we manage then? We did, because we didn't see what developments were just ahead. The situation is much the same today.

The community and charitable mountain

Here again, the 1990s sees a new age – businesses all over the world are recognising their responsibilities to wider groups. The age of 'Good Corporate Citizenship' is with us. This, in turn, means that those who wish to work in the 'caring' services, from the community to the charities, can get their message across, hopefully with more reward and recognition for their enormous and worthwhile efforts. And so, climbing particular mountains in these areas now appears less daunting.

There are many among us who do find it rewarding to be working in the 'caring' areas. Examples include fundraising for a national charity concerned to bring a better quality of life to those who are both deaf and dumb, or helping to bring life-preserving supplies of food and other aid to starving populations in a continent like Africa or India. Yet again, others feel it is important to give a share of their time and rare talent to help raise money through organising huge and international charity events. They all need the support of other, more modest, people who service the large number of administrative tasks needed to bring their projects to a successful conclusion – both in terms of quality and in terms of raising the required level of finance for the selected good cause.

Getting to the top can be equally rewarding in all these spheres. What is important, though, is to decide which is the right way ahead for you. Most of the distinguished people who helped in the research for this book emphasised this point, saying that the earlier in life a decision is taken as to the area in which an individual wishes to spend their working life, the better. Even if a mistake is made, it can be rectified. What is too expensive to contemplate is the wastage involved in time spent in an area of work which is not fulfilling, not satisfying or rewarding in all senses of those words.

It is important, too, to be mindful of the 'human' aspects and priorities. Lady (Judith) Wilcox, previously a successful businesswoman and currently chairperson of the National Consumer Council, puts it this way, 'I would like ... to think that I've been able to reassure the timid that not only the noisy make it – all the way.'

Another highly successful woman, best-selling author Jilly Cooper, comments on the importance of parental influence, a thread running through comments made by many distinguished people asked about whose opinions were important to them. Jilly says, 'I think I always want my mother to think I've written a good book. That would cheer me up.' Jilly goes on to point out that praise from the professional is 'always the one you want most'.

Asked for advice for the reader she says, 'Charles Clore's, which is "the harder I work, the luckier I get", and I really do think working hard is the way to get to the top.'

But, you are asking, why ten steps? And what are they?

The answer to the first question is simple: the development process has been divided into ten steps because ten steps do not make the task daunting, yet fewer could seem too simple. Ten steps are neat; not too many, not too few – and the principle really works rather well. There is a beginning, a middle and an end! In a strange sort of way life inevitably demands that we go full circle, but that is also what life is about, and it is none the less rewarding and enjoyable for that!

So, what are these ten steps? The steps are set out in Part 2 of this book. The natural place to start is at the beginning. As the Chinese say, a journey of a thousand miles starts with the first step. So it is with this analysis of how to get to the top – in business, the arts or academia. The first step is to decide to do it and to start with the commitment of finding out about yourself.

Step 1 KNOW YOURSELF Helps you to understand the type of person you are, and what you have to offer.

The other steps become more easily identifiable after you have come to grips with the first.

Step 2 SETTING GOALS Assists you to recognise and set you own agenda and goals.

Step 3 GETTING IN (AND OUT) Gives you an insight into what organisations are looking for.

Step 4 GETTING ON Advises you how to understand management priorities, and where and how to get help from peer groups and mentors.

Step 5 SELLING YOURSELF Identifies the factors for success and the importance of commitment, confidence and of having ideas.

Step 6 EARNING YOUR KEEP Discusses current practice in management, identifies the 'alienation factor' and advises on how you can ensure you are 'earning your keep'.

Step 7 ACHIEVING STATUS   Looks at status from many viewpoints and discusses how you can achieve it.

Step 8 INCREASING YOUR VALUE   Covers the importance of taking the wider view, and provides guidance on self-development.

Step 9 MAKING YOUR VOICE HEARD   Addresses the key areas of achieving influence and ensuring you are an effective communicator.

Step 10 THE ASSESSMENT   Points the way ahead and shows how to benefit from the experience and advice of your peers and mentors. Includes tips from influential business people. It also examines the very important question 'Is it worth it?'

This last all-important question is one which each reader must ask and answer for him or herself – what does one do when at the top, when one has achieved what one set out to achieve, and is it worth it? The comments in Step 10, from some distinguished poeple who have made it to the top, will be useful in helping you to decide the issue for yourself.

Part 3 of the book signposts certain key areas and provides worksheets for you to fill in on, for example, self-appraisal on progress you are making, on your skills and experience and their development.

Finally, it is natural that in the early stages of getting to the top, the matter is one of a simple progression, a 'building-block' approach, where each stage has to be passed through before you can progress to the next. As you make progress, however, it is possible to interrelate the stages so that you are making progress on more fronts. For example, even before you have got that important job in the organisation of your choice, it could make very good sense to hone up your communication skills. They will always stand you in good stead. In this book, therefore, you should 'dip' into and out of the areas of most importance and interest, those which you find most relevant and useful in terms of your own particular context at the time.

I do hope you like it and find it helpful.

Marie Jennings

PART TWO

▲

The Ten Steps

STEP 1

▲

KNOW YOURSELF

Getting to the top – of anything – is a matter of positive action, whether you are starting out, or half-way up the ladder. This first step is a very basic one. But it is essential.

Other steps you will find in this book should also be considered at this stage – as you may find it possible to work them alongside this one. Be careful, though, not to attempt too much too soon. 'Learning as you go' is a prudent way to scale your individual mountain.

Taking one step at a time is good advice. In this first step priority is placed on finding out about yourself and what you have to offer; it examines your attitude to risk, together with other factors such as whether or not you are assertive and have good health, and the steps you can take.

So you've decided you'd like to try to get to the top of your particular mountain. What are the key factors involved? You will need, of course, to know yourself – what you are, what you want to put into life, what you want from life – and indeed what aspects of life, and why. This will help you to identify the type of person you are from a selection of personality types. These you will find identified later on in this book. Your strengths, hopes, fears, insecurities, interests, potential and assertiveness should be known. Also your attitude to risk, failure, challenge and pressure. Are you gregarious or introverted? This important question should be answered. What you've got going for you should then be identified as a result. Then the steps you can take thereafter can be spelt out. Understanding whether you are assertive, passive or aggressive is important. You need to know.

Making a Start

It is natural to think that you are special, that you have unique qualities (or perhaps even lack them), that you are gifted to a large degree (or possibly only to a small one). Generally speaking, you may have much to contribute to the world at large, but are not sure how to go about it. This is a view shared by many of us. We believe, especially if we come from small, closely knit and loving family backgrounds, that the world is our oyster, but we are not sure what it consists of.

Well, are we in for a number of surprises!

It is as well to remember that all worlds of work, in business, industry, sports, the arts or academia, are like a series of mountains. You ascend one peak only to find others, and yet others, stretching into the distance, each higher than the last. Contemplating the possibility of scaling these mountains can be a daunting prospect.

To get to the top in terms of financial reward, to become a top business leader, is not for all of us. Some of us may believe that treading the path can lead to a narrowly focused life and that this can be expensive in terms of all the precious time needed to be spent on it!

Most of us want an interesting life, even recognising that it won't be all that easy, and realising that to enjoy the peaks we must endure the agony of the troughs! Most of us accept that we need money to live, but some of us do recognise that money has no value in itself, that it is simply one of several means of exchange for goods or services. What, however, we are all searching for is a sense of fulfilment, or satisfaction, of believing

21

that we are getting the most possible out of life, using to the full the skills and abilities we have. We should all recognise that as a basic objective in our lives.

Some of us, though, do want and even need to accept the challenge of scaling the mountains. We find the exhilaration of the achievement exciting, the heady atmosphere of attempting the impossible (as it seems) and discovering it is achievable is both tempting and often irresistible! To many of us the joy of winning is the food and drink of intellectual satisfaction – we need it, we want it and we seek it.

To achieve what you want from your life you must listen to those around you with wisdom, and take their advice. You need to know yourself – as you really are, with no element of wishful thinking. You need to recognise your strengths and weaknesses. Above all you need to know how ambitious you are, and how to identify your aspirations.

Finding Our About Yourself

Finding out about yourself is not easy. One of the distinguished academics interviewed for this book, Professor Meredith Thring, explained it extremely well to me many years ago. He was making a point that is fundamental to finding out about yourself. He described it as recognising that you have three 'centres', the head, the heart and the hands. Every human being has a need to engage each to the right degree and in the right proportion to release the potential which that person is capable of achieving. But not all of us are aware of the need to balance what we are doing intellectually (the head), with our emotional responses (the heart) and our practical output (the hands), in the right proportions. And how do we know if we have? Well, apparently, we will certainly know if we haven't! We will be feeling frustrated and unhappy, we will believe that our worth isn't recognised where it should be recognised and so on.

So, take that essential first step and find out how you feel. Decide for yourself the proportions out of 100 you would give to your need for intellectual stimulation, for emotional involvement, for practical output.

Where You Stand

Next, it is important to find out where you stand, and relate this to where you want to be, and/or end up. Answering the following questions should help you to find out where you stand, as to your aspirations.

	Yes	No
Would you say you are ambitious?	☐	☐
Very?	☐	☐

What aspirations do you have:

	Yes	No
to run a major commercial enterprise?	☐	☐
to become an entrepreneur?	☐	☐
to run your own business?	☐	☐
to become a millionaire?	☐	☐
to have a reputation as an achiever?	☐	☐
to innovate? (With or without recognition or reward?)	☐	☐
to be known as a top professional?	☐	☐
to be considered as highly ethical?	☐	☐
to become one of the 'great and the good'?	☐	☐
to be a 'top' musician, athlete, artist, designer, parliamentarian, newscaster or in some other specialist field?	☐	☐

Do you like and *need* variety, seeing how a problem-solving technique in one direction can be adapted to provide the solution to a problem in another? ☐☐

Do you like and need to be with people of urge, real ability, direction and motivation – people who have something of importance to contribute (it could be to the world of business, or science, or literature, or art, or philosophy)? ☐☐

23

Do you like to be part of the scene where the people you are with are taking decisions which prompt and promote change, and actually make things happen?

Are you a perfectionist? You will immediately recognise this quality in yourself if you are.

The Be'ers and the Do'ers

Remember that the world is divided into two types of people, those who want to '*be*' something, and those who want to '*do*'. What is important to you is to decide whether *you* want to 'be' or to 'do'. Hopefully you will find the decision easier by the time you have finished reading this book. If you are a 'be' person, you will be looking for recognition, reward in terms of money or status. If you are a 'do' person, the task is the important thing. You will want to know that you have mastered a new technique, solved a problem, created an opportunity.

If the challenge to you is to pioneer a new development or to sharpen and focus planning, then you are one of those who want to 'do' things, or at least to try to do them! Not recognising this simple fact has led to a lot of frustrations for countless people over the years.

The Need for Time

Another point to recognise is that it takes time for a new thought to take root in the minds of others to whom it has been introduced. Many glazed looks on the faces of audiences can be witnessed every day because the thought they are being given is too new and/or radical. It is important to 'slow down' and given people time to come to terms with a new concept. It is equally important to remember that the majority of reactions to a new concept are hostile. Most people simply don't like change, and the fastest and easiest reaction when an answer is called for is 'No'! It is also possible to discern different attitudes among people of different nationalities. For example, many Americans will take a risk with their own money if there is an evens (50 per cent) chance of success in promoting and selling a new product or service, while a British company will still need reassurance − often even if they are provided with evidence that there is a 90 per cent certainty of success! It can be useful to bear such thoughts in mind when discussing a new concept with a US or UK businessperson! Remember also that the Japanese usually plan far into the future; also that many South-East Asians will cut prices very keenly for an order.

The implications of change

Most people hate change, they are frightened of it. Are you? Think about it. Of course money and status are important, but how important are they to you? You need to know this as you make a start on climbing your own particular mountain. (The subject of status will be dealt with in Step 7).

With the world of technology at our feet today, the options for living your life, to achieve the personal satisfaction you want and need, have never been wider. Make sure you make the most of your opportunities. This sort of analysis, and synthesis, is unquestionably the most worthwhile investment of your time.

The Key Components

The type of person you are

What you are, what you want and why should be known to you, *now*. Perhaps it already is, but if not this little SWOT test will help. SWOT stands for Strengths, Weaknesses, Opportunities and Threats. Test yourself by completing these points as they affect you.

Strengths List these.

Weaknesses List these, being honest, even ruthless, if you can.

Opportunities List what you can recognise are the

25

opportunities which may be available to you and where you should look for more.

Threats   List any threats you can identify or any which you feel could be emerging on the horizon.

Stand back and assess the comments you have made against each item to see where you stand. Here is an example:

Bill is a practical man. He lists his strengths as:
seeing practical opportunities;
having a range of practical skills;
being able to get on with his colleagues;
being able to think ahead;
having a good measure of experience in his current job.
But, Bill is frustrated. He believes that he has hit the 'glass ceiling'. Why?

Identifying his weaknesses:
he is not as good as he should be at getting his message across;
he is tongue-tied at committee or during his appraisal interviews;
he is a modest man, so he blends with the furniture in gatherings of people.

Bill's opportunities:
he knows that he is worthy of promotion, that the opportunity is there, but he doesn't know how to grasp it.

Threats for Bill:
being passed over for promotion, time and again.

So what should Bill consider to solve his problems and make the most of his opportunities? At the risk of being over-simplistic, the answer is that Bill should ensure that he 'is visible'. At the present time he is not. His strengths lie in his capacity to do his job, and this will be recognised. What can't be clearly seen are the talents he has to do more, and to contribute more fully to the organisation. His potential 'added value' needs to be clearly visible. Because of his natural modesty, Bill is reluctant to push himself forward. But there are things he could do to help himself. He could read up about how to contribute in a wider sense, how to do better in committees and during appraisal. He could enlist for courses to help him with presentation, writing and other complementary skills to the ones he already has. And he could seek – and find – someone to whom he can relate as a 'role model' or 'mentor'.

If Bill tries to make progress in the areas he has identified as weak he will travel – at least some of the way – down the right path to get the promotion he seeks. In so doing he will be dealing, in a practical sense, with the threat he has recognised, that of being passed over for promotion.

The importance of personality

Another area for you to examine is that of your own personality. It is important to check your personality. If you can accurately identify the qualities in your personality, this should help you to know your reactions better in particular situations which you may be called on to face. Here are some questions to answer which should help you to find out.

	Yes	No
Are you gregarious or introverted?		
Do you find it easy to meet people you don't know and set up a conversation?		
Do people you have just met want to meet up with you again?		
Do you make friends easily – at home or at work?		
Do you have a large circle of friends? Of acquaintances?		
Do you keep in touch with others or expect them always to call you?		

	Yes	No
Are you suspicious and fearful of what you don't know?		
Are you volatile in temperament? Do you frequently 'fly off the handle'?		
Do others look to you for an opinion? For action on a particular issue?		
Are you a leader or a follower?		
Do you laugh easily?		
What opinion do others have of you? Do you know? Can you find out?		
Do you have confidence in yourself, in your ideas and ability to deliver them?		
Do you have special abilities? Special skills? (Refer to Step 3 and Appendix 3 in Part 3 to look in more detail at this area.)		

As a result of answering these questions you should get clear indications as to whether or not you prefer to work closely with people, or whether you are happier and more productive working quietly away in a small and close environment. You should begin to see whether you wish to take more of a lead in things – this matter is dealt with in more detail under Step 7 in this book. You should start to recognise whether or not you have the potential to influence others. All these areas are important in getting to grips with knowing yourself.

It is important to be honest with yourself. Take a leaf out of the book of Dr Alexander King, internationally renowned as a philosophical thinker and practical innovator of wide concepts. He was one of two founders of the Club of Rome which, more than twenty years ago, published a report it had commissioned, *The Limits to Growth*, one of the first works to question where our planet was heading. Dr King says, 'I regard myself as a maverick in official, international and non-governmental activities. I am a compulsive innovator and, although I listen to others and take advice, I hold fast to my objectives. My attitude can be expressed by an aphorism, "They say, you stroke the cat the wrong way. I say, let the cat turn round!".'

Where you stand now

Within this basic area there are many factors which need to be taken into consideration. For example, regarding yourself, it is important to know whether or not you are ambitious, also to be realistic as to where you stand in terms of time. Are you at the beginning of your working life, in mid-career, or coming to the end of what you may consider to be the 'grindstone' of work?

In addition, you need to be able to fill in those other 'grey areas' about yourself. What type of organisation do you want to be in? Do you want to be an entrepreneur? Can you influence others, and indeed do you wish to? Do you find stress a spur or an obstacle and how much stress can you take before you metaphorically 'go bananas?' Do you want a 'steady' job? Are you easily bored? Must you have stimulation? Can you provide it yourself?

Again, the environment in which you can work best needs to be known. Are you someone who sees your particular 'mountain' as climbing to the top in a large organisation, or do you want to run your 'own', smaller outfit? Indeed, are you a more 'private' person, seeking to make your contribution quietly, even perhaps in a sometimes solitary world of your own, polishing up your skills as an artist, a musician, an author or an academic?

And finally, that most important question of all needs to be answered: what do you think is worthwhile; what will represent success to you, and give you a feeling of satisfaction and achievement?

Working through the book, some of your answers to these questions will become clear. In addition you need to define:

What sort of work appeals to you?
   profitable production?
   sales?
   caring (teaching, nursing, probation, etc.)?
   with people? with animals? charities?
   inanimate (e.g mathematics, geology, etc.)?
Busy all the time (e.g. machine-oriented)? With time off
   (e.g. theoretical) or 'work as you please' (e.g. writing, which
   can frequently dominate the author!)?

Take a few minutes to consider these questions and formulate
your answers.

Your attitude to risk

Most important, in terms of stepping-stones to the top, is to
recognise your attitude to risk. Some people are attracted by risk,
some hate it, others fear it. It is as well to know where you stand
on this issue.

  To judge your attitude to risk simply, take a look at the
following questions:

Yes No

How do you assess risk? Does it mean 'losing out'? ☐☐
In financial terms? In terms of status? In terms of
disappointing others at work? At home?

Do you find risk exciting? Is it a tonic to you? ☐☐

Do you look for challenge? ☐☐

Do you 'play safe' as much as possible? ☐☐

Is your money locked up in safe savings and ☐☐
investment options?

Or do you take greater financial ☐☐
risks in the hope of greater rewards?

Is your car one of the safe and steady variety? ☐☐

	Yes	No

Would you say you are a 'safe and steady' driver?

Do you plan holidays a year in advance?

Do you change your job often?

Do you enjoy gambling? Following the horses and/or dogs? Using gambling machines? Taking risks driving? Buying shares?

Answering these questions will give you guidance as to whether your attitude to life is always to seek the safe and cautious route, or whether you are prepared to take a risk. The answers should also help you to identify whether risk is important to you – whether taking a risk adds to the excitement element in your life, whether you need it as much as some people need a drink! At times? Often? Always? You really *do* need to know.

In a related context:

	Yes	No

If you had an unexpected exciting opportunity to change your life dramatically, would you say 'No' immediately on principle?

Would you carefully examine the opportunities?

Would you say 'Yes' in principle, with only a little thought, so as not to let the opportunity pass you by?

Your answers to these questions are important in relation to the progression of your career at work. If you are seen to be keen to explore opportunities, that is a clear steer for those who may be considering giving you more responsibility. The answers will also indicate whether or not you will let that important opportunity slip by because you hadn't noticed it! The window of opportunity generally identifies itself when we least expect it – and it is rarely open for long. If you really 'know yourself' you should immediately identify an opportunity when it is revealed to you. And you should immediately act accordingly – accepting the opportunity if it is right for you, and finding ways of perhaps relating it to what you do want, if you know that it is not 'quite' what you are looking for.

Missed opportunities along the way are experienced by us all. Try to work towards keeping them to a minimum if you can.

The type of personality you have

There are many different types of personality. Identifying your own personality type is critical to your success in 'knowing yourself'. Here is a simple checklist for you to work from.

Are you an extrovert?   In this case you will enjoy being with people, be among the first to respond when your opinion is asked, not be reluctant to put yourself forward.

Are you an introvert?   In this case you will be good at 'keeping yourself to yourself'. You won't give your opinion unless asked. You'll be the last person to put yourself forward.

Are you a positive person?   You will see the bright side of everything, be someone who is keen to say 'Yes', whenever possible, be prepared to accept extra responsibility, new tasks, to explore new horizons.

Are you a negative person?   If you are you will immediately see the problems inherent in anything being explored, have a tendency to say 'No' in principle – to anything which requires extra effort from you. You will be known as someone shirking responsibility wherever possible. You will want everything to stay exactly as it is, because that way is safe and free from hassle. You want to be sure that the ground is under your feet all the time.

It is important to make sure that you know which 'fit' is basically you. The list of 'types you might meet on your way to the top' featured in Part 3 takes a rather lighthearted look at this area, but the issue is a serious one. The type of person you are *does* affect your chances of success, so remember this fact.

Assertiveness

My dictionary defines 'assertiveness' as 'the disposition to bold or confident assertion without need for proof'. It defines assertion as 'confident declaration or affirmation of a statement'. To assert oneself is to 'compel recognition of one's rights or position'.

A simple way of identifying assertive persons is to notice how they behave. Do they talk well? Are they 'positive', and interested in wider issues? These may relate to public debates on national and international affairs, the quality of food, or local issues, for example, the local rail service. Do they initiate discussions? Do they disagree with opinions? Are they always asking the question 'Why'? Are they persistent?

To make the most of your opportunities you should know whether or not you are assertive. And you should recognise the differences between being assertive, being passive and being aggressive.

If you are **assertive**:

> you are direct, honest, open − and you *listen*;
> you can see the other person's point of view;
> you can see the options when there are difficulties, and you can identify the solutions;
> you don't let others sidetrack you, you stick to your point of view, hopefully persuading others to join you;
> you respect others as you wish them to respect you;
> you search for consensus in a situation of conflict;
> you are articulate, expressing your concepts clearly and objectively.

If you are **passive**:

> you go along with the 'crowd';

you don't put your own thoughts forward, you keep them to yourself;

you appear, and perhaps are, indecisive;

even if you see and can assess the damaging results of conflict you still fear 'getting stuck in' to the argument;

you keep yourself to yourself, perhaps building up inside you levels of anger and frustration;

you avoid speaking up – and sometimes can't articulate your case;

you won't do anything about any of these factors.

If you are **aggressive**:

you can't – or won't – see any other person's point of view;

you *know* you are 'right' and won't listen;

you set out to bend everybody else to your will;

you *must* win – every issue, every time;

you can't see what you may be losing as a result.

Sorting out whether you are assertive, passive or aggressive – honestly – is an important step on your way to 'knowing yourself'. Don't be alarmed if the reckoning you make is less than complimentary! Just decide that it is time to get stuck in and do something about it!

You can train yourself to be more assertive. This does not mean that you will be manipulating others for your own gain: rather that you will be achieving more control of yourself, to become less shy and more expressive. This will, in turn, help to influence the way others behave towards you, especially those who could mistreat you.

Assertiveness training relates to speaking up about interpersonal difficulties and helping to resolve problems. So how do you set about this? A simple starting point is to talk to close friends on the subject. Before you do so, decide for yourself whether they are assertive or not. Be direct. Discuss the matter with them. It could be as helpful to them as it should be for you.

If you want to go further there are now many books on the subject to be found in local libraries and bookshops (see Bibliography). And if you want to really study the subject the management and educational bodies should be able to help with signposting suitable courses which will include self-assertion. Contact The Institute of Directors, The British Institute of Management, The Institute of Personnel Management, The Industrial Society, The Trades Union Congress or the business management department of your local university and/or polytechnic.

So how can you become more assertive? Here are four simple rules to follow.

> Make sure that you are a good listener. Check up on this. It is really important.
>
> Ensure you really *understand* the case which is being made to you. Check this out.
>
> Make your points clearly and objectively.
>
> Identify the desired results − and their consequences.

Bear in mind that though assertiveness may be easy to define in theory, it is difficult to achieve it sensibly in practice. Don't be put off. Stick with it. It can reward you with worthwhile results.

The courtesy factor

Courtesy is very important. It is often taken for granted. We all like to think we are very courteous and considerate. But are we? Check your courtesy count by answering these questions.

	Yes	No
If you are invited for a meal out − to a restaurant or a friend's home − do you send a letter or make a phone call of thanks afterwards?		
Do you acknowledge birthday cards and Christmas or birthday presents?		
Do you view apology as a sign of weakness?		
Are you aware of the birthdays of those you work with?		

	Yes	No
Do you view asking for help as a defeat?		
Do you view aggressive behaviour as a virtue? Or a vice?		
Do you give praise – often and easily?		
Are you really as fair as you think you are?		
Are you a good listener?		
Do you value and practise 'good manners'?		
How positive is your negative? Do you say 'No' courteously and kindly?		
Are you prepared to take an interest in other people's problems?		
Does your body language (signs of irritation, boredom, fear, anxiety) say things about you which you would rather keep from others?		

The answers to these questions will give you an indication of how courteous you are and how you respond to the needs of others. Increasing your positive courtesy factor can help you enormously on your way to the top.

You should, however, be very clear about why you are (or want to be) courteous. Is this for your own satisfaction and comfort, or is it to ensure that you make progress in your own plan of things? Being sincere in your courtesy really does count.

The health factor

As you are assessing yourself, do remember to assess the physical factors as well. They are important. If you really wish to reach for the top in a competitive world you will need to recognise the quality of your overall health and mental stamina, your physical stamina, your attitude to physical exertion, your intellectual urge and motivation; all these play their part in the degree of success you will be able to achieve. Here is a short checklist which should help.

Health Is this good? Are you prone to illness? Have you suffered from serious illness?

Physical stamina Do you have this? To a high degree? Could you continue to work effectively without, say, much sleep over periods of three days or more?

Physical exertion Are you lazy or energetic? Do you take exercise regularly? Are your hobbies sedentary or 'outside' hobbies?

Mind Do you find it easy to relax – with crosswords etc. or are you always thinking and/or 'doing' things?

Your health is a very important factor if you are striving for the top. Many prominent industrialists rate it as *the* most important factor. You need to ensure that you are energetic, highly motivated, have the health and strength to cope with stress, can relax – when you have the time, and above all, that you can work hard and long hours, over long periods, without finding that it clouds your judgement and gives cause for concern for your colleagues at work, or your family at home.

It is important to know where you stand on the issue of health. Then relate this to the world of work to ensure that your efforts in this area reflect what is right for you.

Evaluation and Education

Steps you could take

Some of the key areas you should examine have been identified. Note down the comments you have made about yourself against each area. Study them.

The next step should be to check out the accuracy of your evaluation. Talk to others whose opinions you respect. If you can, do this openly and seriously, offering to do as much for them, if they would find it useful. If you can't approach the matter openly, don't abandon the task. Check on the questions you want to ask the relevant persons, separate them into 'bite-size' bits and ask them in code. A question posed to a friend or colleague, like 'I find you a very positive person, you are always offering to do things, seeing the bright silver lining to the cloud. For myself, I'd like to know whether you see me as a positive, or a negative person ...' should elicit an answer which you may not like, but which is very useful to you in the context of knowing yourself better.

Study the comments you have assembled and make yourself an action plan for the future. A useful way is to see yourself as 'You Ltd' and apply some of the criteria which may be familiar to you in business, and which are set out in this book, step by step. You will find the 'Action Plan for You Ltd' set out in Part 3. Work with it and then set out a time-scale against what you want to achieve. It is very important to recognise that any task ideally has a beginning, a middle and an end. Recognise this in your approach to getting to 'know yourself'.

Success

Success is really what it is all about.

Being a success is wonderful. It boosts your confidence, invigorates you, encourages you to more and greater successes in your life. To know yourself you should identify what success means to you. You need to define your own recipe for success.

Here are some different types of success. Success means:

- achieving your own personal goals;
- being promoted, consistently, at work;
- making a lot of money;
- becoming a public figure;
- achieving recognition in business and industry, the world of art, literature, science etc.;
- making things happen in your own sphere;
- creating new concepts, innovations, processes;
- being popular;

- becoming a leader;
- being happy — in your work, at home, at leisure.

Identifying the elements of success which are important for you from this list will help you to create your own recipe for success. Do it. Today.

Finally, here are two pieces of advice. First from the Baroness Platt of Writtle, distinguished engineer and former chairperson of the Equal Opportunities Commission — 'Work hard, do your homework, however difficult, and above all keep your sense of humour!' And from David Wickes, international television and film producer — 'Remember retirement is a non-concept for creative people.'

Remember

- Knowing yourself as you really are is the key to getting what you want from your life and a stepping-stone to achieving your personal 'top'.

- Building on your strengths and working on your weaknesses is well worth the effort.

- Finding out what others think about you can be valuable.

- Your health, and whether this is good or not, is an important factor.

- Courtesy is a most useful attribute — recognised more often than you may think.

- Success — at whatever you wish to achieve — is within your grasp. However, it is up to you to know what you want, and to set high personal standards to achieve your potential.

- You need to identify whether or not you want to compete, to reach a plateau, to challenge others, or create your own market.

- You need to know *why* you want:
  influence;
  power;
  money.

STEP 2

—▲—

SETTING GOALS

To know yourself is the essential first step to the top. You examined the key issues in Step 1. As a result you should know more about yourself and what you have to offer.

In Step 2 you must set your goals and recognise your agenda to get to the top.

This step looks at the important aspects of where you stand at the moment: your objectives, whether or not you are creative and can cope with stress; and how to set your goals for the type of success you are looking for.

There are many important questions to ask yourself before you can make any real sense out of setting your goals. First, you must know where you are at the moment; then you must decide where you are likely to be going on your present path; next you must be sure of where you would like to be going; and finally you should have at least a glimpse of where, ideally, you want to end up.

There is much to learn from the experiences of others. Peter Hayes, a successful businessman, puts it this way – 'It was important for me to do the job which I do better than anyone else and, as far as I can judge, I have achieved that. I do think there is much more to achieve and I define the goal as being to get the true value of achievement, rather than its monetary expression, accepted as the benchmark for success by many.' Dr Alexander King gives a slightly different gloss with his perception. He says, 'The primary need is to have a clearly formulated view of one's goals and objectives and then an unwavering persistence towards their accomplishment. In this life, if one has no clear vision of what one wants, the probability of getting anywhere, to say nothing of the top, is remote.'

Where You Stand at the Moment

Step 1 will have helped you to determine where you stand at the moment. In this second step we need to look at the matter in more detail. This questionnaire will help you to find out more about the direction in which you should take your next steps.

Assuming you are happy in your choice of work, you will need to know how to consolidate your position and improve it. You therefore need to identify the following.

	Yes	No
Do you know when your next promotion or move will take place?		
Are you happy with the level of progress you are making?		
Can you yet identify where you want to end up? At the top of the organisation? As a department head? As a known and respected specialist?		
Do you need to make a career change?		

All the above questions lead to the key issue of whether or not you have defined your career objectives.

This is a very important question. Many people start with determining this at the beginning of their business or professional lives. Others do not. They are happy to wait to see how fate deals with them and to take decisions as the need arises.

But the question is still a very valid one in terms of what you want to get out of your life. For example, if you are of mature years and in mid-career, now is the time to start thinking of what you want to do with the rest of your life. Today, many of us consider it important to make a career change in our late forties or early fifties, preparing for a more relaxing and leisurely existence. This necessitates early-warning information with regard to your priorities on planning for the future, and for retirement.

Others of us, while young, need to ensure that we will be able to realise our ambitions and achieve the personal objectives we have set for ourselves, no matter how ambitious these may appear to be on the surface.

Career Objectives

Step 1 will have helped you to come to some early conclusions. In order to help you to refine your career objectives further, the following examples may be helpful.

Some career objectives in a business/industry environment:
- to be perceived and valued as a competent manager;
- to be valued as a key member of the team;
- to be recognised as a business leader;
- to be valued as an innovator;
- to be recognised as a stable and consistent member of staff.

Some career objectives in a professional and academic environment:
- to be recognised as a 'leader' in the sector;
- to be valued for new and innovative thinking;
- to be identified as an opinion-former;
- to achieve a reputation for quality in work;
- to be known as someone concerned for the quality of life of colleagues, someone they can rely on for help;
- to be valued as someone who can bring differing colleagues together.

Some career objectives for being your own boss:
- to build a large and successful organisation;
- to build an organisation known as a quality player in a chosen 'niche' market;

- to get very rich;
- to innovate in your own organisation;
- to have fun and satisfaction in being your own boss.

All this can be summed up and crystallised, perhaps, in this short and succinct phrase: 'To be known as someone to be relied on to make things happen'.

In the words of Vincent Duggleby, a leading broadcaster on personal finance, 'The ability to make decisions at the right time and with confidence is one of the most important, if not the most important attributes.' So, if you are blessed with this ability, recognise it and develop it.

The career objectives set out above should help you in some measure to determine what you are aiming for. Use them to write down your own career objectives, specifying in as much detail as you can what your aims are, and what you are seeking to achieve.

Other factors of importance in getting to know where you stand, can provide a useful guideline:

	Yes	No
Do you find stress a spur? Do you enjoy a challenge?		
Does the 'adrenalin' stimulation excite you? Trying to achieve something important and new always produces stress. Remember this. Recognise how it may affect you and plan how you will cope with it. (We will look at stress in more detail on page 51.)		
Do you like or hate working in a team?		
Do you like or hate committee work?		
Do you like or hate deadlines?		
Do you appreciate or dislike the 'discipline' and repetition of administration and/or management?		

It has to be said that if you have an inspiring 'team leader', then team effort can be most exciting and rewarding. It all depends on the members of the team.

Consensus is, of course, important, but reaching it can be time-consuming and is, sometimes, just deadly boring. Frequently, it is a most expensive use of that important commodity, time. Enlightened managements do, of course, recognise this and plan accordingly. Much depends on the effectiveness of putting up the right project in the right way at the right time.

Are you a loner? Some of us are, and some of us just don't recognise the fact until later on, sometimes too late.

The excitement of doing things which are genuinely creative is a very private joy – you keep it to yourself to enjoy it most. It is sad to have to acknowledge that most of business and industry still does not value the potential in the people who are truly creative. They still tend to put them in the box marked 'awkward' – and move them into an area of minimal real power, such as strategic planning. Here they may have current and potential influence and their creative concepts can be put on one side and examined for future use. They are thought to be safely tucked away from where the action is! Of course not everyone needs to be truly creative – but those who are, should be properly appreciated.

Achieving what is worthwhile is the objective – the personal 'mountain' to be climbed as far as all of us are concerned. The time is wasted if what is produced in the end does not have a value – for yourself and for others too.

So, in setting your goals, you need to look at certain key areas in detail. You need to know what you have to offer, and you need to know what you wish to put into and get out of, the world of work.

Let us look at some of these areas.

The importance of creativity

It is important – and relevant – to discover whether or not you are creative. If you are creative you should recognise that there is an inbuilt need in you to express this in ways that give you satisfaction. Bottling it up leads to frustration. It is rather like putting a stopper on a bottle of fizzy drink at the wrong time. The fizz needs to get out and frequently will release the stopper at the most awkward moment!

So how do you discover whether or not you are creative? This checklist should help you to find out.

	Yes	No
Are you imaginative?		
Have you got creative skills? In painting? Gardening? Cooking? Technology? Management? Marketing?		
Do you tend to follow others in their thinking?		
Do you tend to produce imaginative solutions to problems?		
Do you see opportunities where others do not?		
Are you curious to find out things that you don't know?		
Do you like experimenting?		
Do you take risks? Do you assess them?		

If you are creative, it is worth remembering that credit is rarely given to the person who created an important and radical new concept. It is often snatched by others. When you first start out on this route this hurts, then you become blasé about it. In the end you can protect your ego by recognising that if someone has taken your concept, has used it, has denied credit to you, and yes, has stolen your intellectual property, this could mean that that person is impoverished intellectually. He or she has not got the ability to be creative. And the joy of being creative is that you will always know that you can fish again in the pool – developing a number of new ideas and new concepts on which you can work to rediscover again the excitement of creating something worthwhile.

But you should only follow this road if you can truthfully say that you won't be soured by the experiences you will encounter, and that you honestly put the financial rewards, which may be denied to you, and which may be enjoyed by others, as matters of secondary importance, and of no major significance in your scheme of things.

45

Skills

Of course, what you bring to the party in terms of skills is critical. Frequently we indulge in some wishful thinking when we sit down to assess our skills! This is dangerous.

Skill is really related to your expertise in one or more areas. It defines the practised ability you have, the facility you bring to bear in doing something. It can also relate to your dexterity and even to the level of tact you have.

So it is important for you to assess just how skilful you are, and in which areas. (You will find the matter of the skills required for different tasks and jobs dealt with in Part 3 Appendix 3.)

The importance of teams and teamwork

Some people positively enjoy teamwork and the 'buzz' that comes from being a member of a team. Being a member of a team that is achieving progress can be stimulating and exciting in a different way from 'doing your own thing'. There is enjoyment in sharing, in jointly acquiring knowledge, in using the abilities of some members of the team to stimulate the abilities in others. When the team is failing, then several members of it should support the faint-hearted – and ensure that success can be achieved.

It is important and relevant to know whether or not you are good at teamwork. This checklist should help in this context.

	Yes	No
Do you like being by yourself, or do you seek the company of others?		
Do you like working alone?		
Do you find it difficult to concentrate when others are in the same room?		
Have you got a good sense of timing? Do you recognise that when you are in a meeting there is a need for decision-making within time constraints?		

Yes No

Do you give a priority to reaching consensus decisions or are you keen to study an area, come to conclusions, reach a decision and then seek to persuade others to your point of view?

Do you like being with people, all the time?

Do you always seek other opinions and advice for personal decisions you may be making?

Noting down your answers to the questions posed above should give you a clear indication of whether or not you like working with others in teams. In this case, ensure that you make this known as soon as possible to those who may be able to influence your progress. If you believe you are not at your best in teamwork, then recognise this, and either see what you can do to improve the position, or seek opportunities where you can work more by yourself.

The importance of the type of work and work environment

The type of work you do is very relevant. Ensuring you are working in an environment in which you can express yourself and use your skills is the key to the contribution you will be able to make in your working life. You should remember that, in the round, we are expected currently to work for seven hours a day, for five days a week, for forty years of our lives! Admittedly we have time off for holidays etc., but it is still a daunting prospect. Just consider how much more daunting it is if you are committed to doing things at work in an environment you don't like, with people you don't respect and can't get on with. The thought presents a gloomy picture to say the least.

So it is important for you to decide the type of work which interests you and the type of work environment which is right for you.

Type of Work

We are all different, so naturally we need to study the type of work which we may find fulfilling. This can break down to the following simple classification:

intellectual work – the head;
practical work – the hands;
emotional work – the heart.

Professor Meredith Thring, a distinguished academic, has spelt out in many books and lectures how important it is that people should use each component of the head, the heart and the hands in the right balance for that person in order to secure a happy and satisfied life with an absence of aggression, and other similar and debilitating consequences. It follows that it is important to consider which comes first in your own case – the area you give the highest priority. If you seek that type of work you should find it offers the satisfaction and fulfilment you seek and need from work.

The following short list identifies the types of work and work environment offered in each category. You can easily extend this list to the categories in which you are interested:

Intellectual – Working in an 'office', 'study' or 'academic' environment. The output is words or figures on computer or paper, interlaced with discussion sessions, lecture or conference platforms. The input is thought, analysis, research, towards development of new patterns of thinking, planning, implementation in the chosen area of activity.

Practical – Working in a factory, office or outside environment on projects involving management, production, 'making' in all senses of the word, in the chosen area of activity. There is much work and thought needed, to continue to improve the process – and for all except craftsmen and those working in production, the output will largely be reports on paper.

Emotional – Working with people, in an inside or outside environment. The chosen area of activity can relate to helping them to use their skills and abilities to better effect, in educational and counselling functions. The output is primarily the effect on people – but frequently combined with reports on paper.

Success

Before you can set your own goals, you should take a look at the subject of success. What does success mean for you?

The *Concise Oxford Dictionary* defines success as 'accomplishment of end aimed at'. This, therefore, means that you must have an 'end', a 'goal', or a series of goals. Some of your goals may be financial, or relate to status, or preferment at work. Others may be more personal, relating to satisfying your own criteria, living up to the standards which you have set yourself. These can be in a much wider context, perhaps in terms of quality of life, helping others, raising the 'larger' issues affecting lifestyle, education, the environment.

It would be very useful to define what you mean by success. Try it. Put down on paper, say, 50–100 words. Here is an example which you may care to use to help you create your own definition.

Success to me means working in a happy, friendly environment. It means being properly rewarded for the effort I make to help the organisation I work for. It means working with and for people who recognise the nature of the contribution I make. It means satisfaction in knowing that my voice will be heard where appropriate, and that I will be given opportunities to progress where possible.

The fifteen minutes or so you spend working out your definition of success as you see it should prove a worthwhile investment of your time.

So, what is success?

Success is really what it is all about.

Being a success is wonderful. It boosts your confidence, invigorates you, encourages you to more and greater successes in your life. To know yourself you should identify what success means to you. You need to define your own recipe for success. Here are some different types of success. Success means:

achieving your own personal goals;
being promoted, consistently, at work;
making a lot of money;
becoming a public figure;
achieving recognition in business and industry, the world of art, literature, science etc;
making things happen in your own sphere;
creating new concepts, innovations, processes;
being popular;
becoming a leader;
being happy – in your work, at home, at leisure.

Identifying the elements of success which are important for you from this list will help you to create your own recipe for success. Do it. Today.

Rules for success

So, what are the rules for success? This is how Sir Denys Henderson, Chairman of ICI, one of the UK's largest and most successful companies, advises the readers of this book to reach for success:

'There is so much in a lifetime career that simply cannot be preordained, I therefore emphasise at the outset that luck will play a big part in the initial choice of job and even more so in subsequent progress. But, equally, you can always shape your own good fortune to some extent by a combination of energy, hard work, resilience and at least a degree of opportunism.

'Do not be afraid to move on to other things if the first choice does not work out – there are only a very select few, in my experience, who have such a strong vocation that they find fulfilment in one single occupation for life.

'Whichever route your career eventually takes, make absolutely certain that there is adequate time for family life and that in carrying out your responsibilities, your personal and professional integrity remain inviolate. However difficult the decision you have to take, it is important to be able to face yourself in the morning satisfied that you have betrayed neither your own principles nor acceptable standards of behaviour.

'If you should choose to exercise your professional skills in industry, above all, aim to enjoy the experience – I certainly have and if I could turn the clock back thirty-four years to when I first joined ICI, I would do it all again.

'Here are my own twelve rules for success:

- If you can, start with a good degree, a good educational background;
- Do the job you are given well;
- Obtain as much experience as you can;
- Ask yourself if you have the stamina it needs (at the top you must always be on the line very early in the morning, no matter what you've been up to the night before . . . not that I nowadays have any nights before!);
- Be curious about things;
- Ask yourself constantly how you can do better;
- Keep your sense of humour, which you must have to start with;
- Cultivate a stable family life;
- Develop strategic vision;
- Make things happen (I meet cleverer people than myself but very often they cannot make things happen);
- Have the necessary courage to take tough decisions;
- Maintain your integrity – personal and professional.'

The Stress Factor

Stress, and whether or not you can cope with it, is an important factor to examine before you can set your personal goals. It is important to know where you stand on this issue.

What causes stress?

There are as many different causes of stress as there are individual sufferers from it. Pressures affect each of us in different ways. Common causes of stress are career problems, financial worries, relationship difficulties, disputes with families friends and neighbours, legal problems, harassment, health.

Any of these can lead to a lack of interest in your work, and a reduction in job satisfaction. You should remember that self-confidence is an essential component for a successful working life. This can be badly eroded if there is more stress than you can handle. As a result progress is impeded and your life at work, with your managers and colleagues, will become increasingly difficult.

In essence, stress is the result of a lack of personal 'power', a lack of ability to cope with the situation in hand.

Symptoms of stress

Some of these, as the pressure mounts, can be physical.
Some examples:

> headaches;
> aches and pains.

Other symptoms can be psychological.
Some examples:

> changes in habits, appetite and personal appearance;
> sexual problems;
> bad temper;
> aggressive behaviour;
> general fatigue.

Dealing with stress

So, if you feel that you are suffering from stress, how do you cope?

You will probably feel overwhelmed by your situation, but once you recognise that stress is the cause, you are on your way to dealing with your problem. In this case, you should talk the matter over with family, friends and colleagues at work. Try to give yourself a break, a 'cooling-off' period. If you feel this doesn't help, it is time to consult the experts, in the form of your local doctor, and the medical officer at work if you have one.

There is really no stigma attached to suffering from stress. It is just one of those things. What is important is to recognise whether or not it is a factor in your working life and, if it is, to deal with it appropriately. It could mean that you need to work in a stress-free environment. If this is the case, take a decision to seek one. It could also mean that the stress is caused by a temporary situation. If this is the case, recognise it, and wait for the position to resolve itself.

Positive aspects of stress

Don't be depressed if you believe you are suffering from stress. Remember that many people find they can turn stress to positive advantage. Just think of the people you know who may say to you, in a situation of tension or excitement, 'I can feel the adrenalin running through my veins' – this is stress turned to positive advantage. Many famous actors and actresses are on record as saying that they are extremely nervous before going out on stage. Many well-known international politicians, similarly, are honest enough to admit that they suffer tension and stress before making a major speech or taking part in a national television debate. It is human, and admirable, to want to give of your best. The person who is smugly confident and sanctimonious, and who makes no preparation for an important occasion, is indicating contempt for those he or she may be addressing.

So stress can be good, it can help you to stretch up to achieve what you may hardly have dreamed was achievable. Look it fairly and squarely in the face. The excitement and tension you may feel is a fact to indicate that you are being stretched, and sometimes that can be most positively for the best as far as you are concerned.

So, if someone asks you to attempt the impossible, don't automatically consider it a bore, or an imposition. Look at the opportunity and where it may lead. It could be the most worthwhile opportunity you have been offered for a long time and you should grasp it with both hands.

Levels of Responsibility

Related to the matter of stress is the complementary area of levels of responsibility. It is important for you to know which level is right for you, where you will feel comfortable and at ease. This can be broken down as follows.

Decision-making – a 'top' level of responsibility. This brings with it risks, responsibility (for finance, for others at work, perhaps for safety, for meeting acute time and other schedules).

Middle management – here the level of risk will be less. You will be responsible for following through the decision-making of others. You will need to interpret, administer and deliver the detailed programme as set down and agreed by your bosses.

Operational – here you will be involved in the implementation of the work schedules as laid down by the leaders and the managers. That is not to say that the tasks won't be fulfilling and satisfying in the personal sense. It simply means that you will not be involved in the decision-making and management aspects. At this level the stress factor involved should be minimal.

Relate these levels of responsibility to your situation and decide where you are at the moment. If you are on the operational tier, decide whether or not you want to progress to the managerial tier. If you are on the managerial tier decide whether or not you would be comfortable if you were promoted to the top, the decision-making tier. It could be wise to resist promotion if it means that you will be worried and unable to cope with the stress which that level of responsibility inevitably brings with it. Reading this book should help you to recognise that opportunities should be grasped in the vast majority of cases. Isolate the very few occasions when it may not be right for you and recognise that you should seek your opportunities for success in other areas.

Goals

One matter to settle is whether or not you do have a specific goal in sight. It is helpful if you have, but natural – and in keeping with the majority of human beings – if you haven't.

Nevertheless, it is useful to consider the overall subject of goals. Then at least you will be able to find out where you stand. Try

asking yourself the following questions, noting down the answers.
For the immediate future − say this year and next − ask:

Am I content with my life?
Am I content and happy at work?
Do I want to change things in this period?
    My life?
    My job?
Why?
What needs to be done?

For the medium-term future − say over the next five years:

Ideally, where would I like to be?
    In terms of my life?
    In terms of work?
    In terms of lifestyle?

For the long term − say after the next ten years:

What would I like to have achieved, or be on my way to achieving?
    In terms of my life?
    In terms of work?
    In terms of lifestyle?

If you have filled in your answers to the questions above, you will then have a clearer picture of your goals. Some of them may seem unrealistic, but don't be put off. You must know what you wish to achieve before you can have any possibility of achieving a goal. Even if you don't achieve it 100 per cent, you will, in all probability, achieve it in large measure and this should give you substantial satisfaction.

Remember also that if you don't believe absolutely that you can reach the top, no one else will believe it either. In this context write down your dreams/aspirations and keep checking on them, especially on bad days!

Janet Brady, managing director of a public affairs company, has this advice:

− 'pay attention to your health and state of mind so you can stay at the top once you are there;

- be generous in spirit and share with others around you –
your success becomes theirs and reaps greater rewards;
- never allow someone else to control the money;
- always take time to know what's going on;
- never isolate yourself from reality;
- treat people the way you would wish to be treated;
- never believe your own publicity.'

Personal environment

It is also very important, in setting goals, to be clear about your priorities in relation to your personal environment. For example, what is the priority you give to your work over your home life, or vice versa? Mark them in percentages. If you discover that being at home to cope with the garden and the family means that you like leaving work on time and resent having to stay late or start early, mark Home Life at 60 per cent or more and give Work 40 per cent or less.

If you feel success is very important to you, also that the approval of your peers at work means more to you than the approval of members of your family, acknowledge this fact.

Above all, if you feel you suffer from a conflict between your loyalty to your family and your loyalties at work, recognise that you have a problem and that the sooner you set about resolving it, the better – for your family and for your colleagues at work. You will need to determine how to do this to best effect.

Influencing others

This is another key component to study in relation to setting your goals. The subject of influence is dealt with in more detail in Step 9. What you must seek to establish now is, simply, whether you can or cannot influence others, whether or not you seek to do so, and also, the reverse side of the coin, whether you, yourself, are easily influenced by others or not. How you set about deciding this is important and relevant.

One simple way is to try to remember and identify three occasions when you sought to influence others. Perhaps you tried to persuade them to your point of view in relation to a specific issue, either at home or at work? Or you may have differed from their opinions in relation to a current affairs issue, and in the resulting discussion they came round to your point of view. If you can't remember a specific case, then test the theory out. Raise an issue on which you believe others may take the opposite point of view and see whether or not you can make them change their minds!

And be aware of the opposite side of the coin – where you may have changed sides in a discussion as a result of being influenced by the point of view of others. Was it sensible to have done so? (It may have been.)

In this context, too, it is important to recognise whether you are stimulated by, or back off from, discussions where two points of view are being presented forcibly. Some people do. We can all remember the time when we perhaps disagreed violently with someone in a discussion, but came to the conclusion that discretion was the better part of valour! But those cases can be different. What you should recognise is whether or not you are influenced by the opinion of the last person you were speaking to on a particular issue. Many people are!

In relation to your steps to the top it really is important to find out if you can influence others, if you like doing it, if you do it for the right and proper reasons. If you are positive on all these points this can be of very real benefit to you for the future. Be aware of it.

Be aware, too, if you feel you are not positive on all these points. If you feel that you *want* to improve your powers of persuasion and influence, how do you set about it? The simplest way is to look around you, among your circle of friends, your colleagues at work. Identify the person you know who is a 'persuader', whose opinions matter and are sought, who is listened to. Then study the techniques they use. It could be that the person has that important 'light touch', is amusing to be with, has outrageous views, and is stylish and pithy. It could be that the person is amazingly well read, is right spot up-to-date on current affairs, and knows all the latest gossip.

The techniques which can be used are many and can be identified. How they are applied is the important and subtle aspect which makes all the difference to the end result. Think about it.

Use your eyes and ears and you will find you can turn it into a worthwhile 'game' as a result. For example, in any large group there is always at least one woman whose technique is always to flatter everyone about their appearance. If you are a woman, she admires your dress the instant she sees you. You may be wearing an old sack and looking like a frump, but she will always flatter you. If it isn't your dress it may be your hairstyle she praises. If you are a man she may use more engaging techniques that are suitable to you as an individual! If you are a sage she will flatter your brain, or your latest letter in *The Times* . . . The technique will serve her very well – even if it is obvious to the people who know her well and who find it fairly unattractive!

But you can, if you want to, improve your powers of influence. And if you face up to this, and ask for help from those you think may be able to provide it, you may be surprised to find how positive a response you may elicit!

Achievements

At the end of the day setting goals is useless and worthless unless you achieve them.

This is easier said than done. But there is a simple rule of thumb which you can follow. At least if you have set your goals, for the short, medium and long term, you have recognised their importance and relevance, and know what they are. Then, as a matter of practicality, you can consider, from time to time, what progress you are making. Perhaps it may not be possible to achieve all the goals you have set, but at least you have a better chance of making progress along that path if you start on it. Apathy is the enemy of achievement. Remember this and you won't go far wrong! Don't give up hope if you don't achieve everything you hoped for. Build upon what you have achieved.

What is Worthwhile?

It is important – in relation to achieving your goals – to decide on what is worthwhile in your terms. This is never easy. You must be clear as to your expectations. For example, worthwhileness must be judged in relation to the achievement, taking into consideration the costs, in terms of time and money, as well as what else may have had to be sacrificed to the effort made towards the achievement. 'Is it worth it?' This is the question which must be answered with a resounding, 'Yes, of course it has been worth it!' Frequently we travel hopefully towards our desired objective, only to find out that when it is reached it is somehow, unexpectedly, disappointing. Frequently, too, we discover that the sacrifices made on the way — often without thinking, or calculating the costs in time or in emotional terms — make the achievement seem bitter sweet.

So give some serious thought to worthwhileness and decide how you will define this, in your terms, so that you know exactly where you stand.

Finally, here are two important pieces of advice. The first comes from Richard Pring, Professor of Educational Studies, University of Oxford. He says, 'Be clear about the *values* you want to pursue (otherwise the decisions taken may be efficient, but they will be mindless)'. The second from David Wickes, 'Planned ambition can be dangerous, because every setback can seem like a nail in the coffin of success.'

Remember

- It is important to set goals.

- Be realistic.

- Recognise that you must know the priorities you give to your family and to work, and whether there is occasional or permanent conflict between the two.

- Apathy is an often-used alternative to decision-making. Shun it at all costs. It is the most expensive option.

- You need to make as positive a decision to do nothing, as to do something.

- Over the long term you will either achieve your potential or lose out. That result could well be determined — in part at least — by your actions today.

STEP 3

▲

GETTING IN (AND OUT)

> Steps 1 and 2 should have helped you to know more about yourself, where you stand and where you want to go.
>
> In step 3 we look at how you get into the organisation you have selected as being right for your particular needs.
>
> The step includes information on how to get into or out of an organisation: it focuses attention on what organisations are looking for; discusses the importance of competence; identifies the criteria for promotion and gives tips on how to spot a well-run organisation. Additionally the step looks at how you can change jobs gracefully or change direction, and helps with advice if you are faced with redundancy and retirement.

Naturally, much has been written about the overall subject of getting into your first job, changing the type of organisation you are working in, or changing direction in your career. Naturally, too, this important matter is often shrouded in a lot of pompous gobbledegook. You need to cut through this and to be able to see clearly the practical and possible way forward which is right for you, for your particular circumstances.

Even a relatively few years ago the way forward on the career path was dim and misty. It was difficult to see the way ahead.

Admittedly, there was much more job security, if you wanted it or needed it. Most young people had their choice of job, their choice of organisation, their choice of career. Things are very different today.

In today's competitive and uncertain world the individual has to think first, and to analyse what is right for him or her. You need to know in which direction you are seeking to spend your working life, the type of job which will give you the satisfaction, fulfilment and the reward you seek and need. It is also a matter of having a clear idea of what employers may be looking for, and how to present yourself to them in order to stimulate the right reaction and the positive response.

So how do you set about travelling on this important journey?

Priorities

There are some simple and initial priorities to be observed.

The first is the matter of personal standards. If what you have to offer is based on standards which you have set yourself, then – if these are high – you will know that it is unlikely that you will disappoint anyone in your performance of a particular task or project. If it is a matter of acquiring skills, since your individual standards are high, you will acquire high levels of skill and competence. Your personal standards should, therefore, stand you in very good stead with those you wish to impress.

This is a useful formula to remember. It has served many successful people very well over the years.

The second priority to remember is the simple one of being positive and not negative. If you are positive in your attitudes you will find that most people will respond to you. Where possible human beings like to help and to say 'Yes', given the opportunity.

Admittedly, there are those who are negative and whose immediate reaction is to say 'No', but they can be easily identified, if you look for them. And you should find that there are more of the positive people, whom you can identify, and who will help you on your way to the top. Rarely should you encounter a brick wall, if you go about things the right way. That is not to say that you will get everything you are asking for. What you will get will depend on what you have to offer. But if you have high standards, are positive, have relevant concepts and projects to suggest, and seek a positive person to present them to, then you should find the way forward easier and smoother than you might have thought!

Remember that when you want things done you should ask a busy person! Many successful people have discovered the truth in this saying.

But, all the time, you should remember that the most important factor is to be yourself and not to try to pretend to be something you are not. Shakespeare put it uniquely:

'This above all: to thine own self be true,
And it must follow, as the night the day,
Thou canst not then be false to any man.'

Hamlet iii, 58

'Getting in' for many, means presenting themselves in the right way, sending out the right messages, with the right attitude, and at the right time, addressed to the **right person**. This may be a gross over-simplification but the basic formula can work very well indeed.

The Key Components

For most of us, a traditional and structural path may be the right way ahead. So how do you 'get in' to a blue-chip company? And what is the view they take, from the very different side of the fence where they stand? What are they looking for and how do they handle the overall subject of recruitment and career development?

What the different types of organisations are looking for

Organisations you may want to work for come in all shapes and sizes. At one end of the scale you have the large multinational, the conglomerate with hundreds of thousands of employees in sometimes more than a hundred countries. In such cases the organisation is divided into literally hundreds of different parts, some of which may be involved in maintaining the structure and stability of whole countries in a remote part of the world.

At the other end of the scale you have the small, and sometimes very small, business which provides a living for the proprietor and two or three employees.

In between there are so many different types of organisation, from the manufacturer to the distributor, from the service organisation to the co-operative efforts of craftspeople working in a tranquil collective in a beautiful village in the country, from family companies with a long record of tradition, to the new 'high tech' conglomerates . . .

It is natural to think, perhaps, that the requirements of a blue-chip company, quoted on the world's stockmarkets, may be very different from the qualities sought by a small niche player, or a regional craft-oriented business, but are they?

All organisations are looking, in some measure, for the same elements in the people working for them. They are looking for commitment, integrity, honesty, loyalty, common sense, conscientiousness. This broad brush requirement can be supplemented by many other requirements. In certain cases this will be overlaid by the specialist needs of that particular organisation. But the cornerstone requirements of people will be similar, for without them the structure is built on shifting sands.

What organisations are looking for in new employees

The points made below give a distillation of views from managements of organisations, large and small. They come from a varied group of manufacturers, retailers, service organisations and marketeers.

In general, the essential quality which managements are looking for in the individual is:

a desire for self-development.

They seek the person for whom the job in question will be challenging, and where, in doing it, the person will develop a new and additional level of competence, coming out of it as a better operator at whatever level of work they are undertaking. Naturally, different jobs require differing amounts of skill. These skills are split between two areas, namely technical skill and behavioural skill. If a person has a specific technical skill, then, even if he or she is a touch 'awkward', the management may well decide to put up with that – it may be worth it. Where the job in question is management oriented, then naturally the technical side is less important and the managerial competences take a higher priority. Every job requires a mix of the two.

In all cases, and at all levels, the desire of the individual for self-development is a critical factor. In India they have a saying 'Long time dead' – the person who is not developing all the time is, in fact, losing ground. In terms of the organisation, their contribution is less than 'positive', even negative. In terms of the company's required and essential rate of progress, intellectually they could be considered 'dead'! It is a sobering thought, but it is a relevant one.

In today's economic climate, managements are looking increasingly for the individual who can walk in with a minimum amount of training, and immediately add something of value to the job to be done, and in so doing, to the company. They will be seeking, in the management development area, to improve that individual's skills, pure and simple. If they can develop the person who has potential, then it follows that the organisation's potential can be developed.

Making the most of yourself

So how do you present yourself to the organisation of your choice? The answers to these questions should guide you on your way: first, decide the type of work you are seeking.

Is this creative? (Working in the area of art, design, writing, concept development, new product development, for example.)

Is this management oriented? (Working in administration, personnel, even accounts, for example.)

Is this function oriented, in which case in which area? (Marketing, sales, research, for example.)

In another area? (Identify this.)

Then decide in which type of organisation you would like to work.

Manufacturing sector?
Distribution/retail sector?
Service sector? (Travel, banking, for example.)
Professions or arts (Identify.)
Other (Identify.)

In answering the above questions you should have narrowed down the areas to identify the fields of most interest to you in your working life. Let us say that you have opted to work in marketing in a clearing bank, for example. What should you expect?

A major clearing bank will be looking closely at your levels of skills and abilities when they recruit you. They will be looking at how competent you are, how easily you learn new techniques, whether or not you have what they call 'conceptual flexibility'. This latter quality is the most sought after, and arguably the most lacking, skill in British industry. A bank – and other major employers – will be seeking it and will value the man or woman who brings it to the company.

So what is 'conceptual flexibility'? It is the ability, when presented with a problem, or an opportunity, to come up with several scenarios which address the issue, and with multiple fall-back positions. The person who has this ability is recognised as one with great potential and that person's career path is planned to reflect this accordingly.

What you have to offer

In this context, therefore, it is important for you to know just exactly what you have to offer. In Part 3 Appendix 3, you will find a specimen form. This relates to defining skills and experience in a job in the financial services area, related to giving financial advice. You will learn the following from studying the form.

Knowledge – the need to state clearly what you know, your knowledge. This is stripped down in detail. For example, in the financial area we are talking about familiarity with detailed procedure; as well as familiarity with the detail of operation of different types of industry and legal and legislative procedures, also managerial techniques.

Skills and activities – here again, the overall area is split down into the different skills. In the financial sector these include planning, identifying needs, presentation and assessment.

Business skills – these are given special emphasis, and will be given emphasis in any area of business activity. In addition, of course, the specialist nature of the business sector needs to be broken down in detail, so that the specific individual's knowledge, experience and/or talents can become visible.

You will find this form very useful. If you are interested in a career in finance, your will need to go through it in detail and fill it in where you can. If your intention is to find a way to the top in another business or professional area, you should try to make your own version of the form, adapting it to fit the area in which you are interested. If you refer to Appendix 6 you will see a specimen of an appraisal form and you should go over this, too, and create its 'mirror image', reflecting your own priorities and interests.

Forms like these are used by employers for three main and important purposes. These are:

to enable self-assessment of training needs and career development;

to assist appraisal of skills of an individual and their development needs;

to enable evaluation of training and education course suitability.

In most cases some five stages of knowledge, skills or experience are identified. You, too, need to identify the levels of your knowledge, skills and/or experience to enable you to get into the organisation of your choice.

Remember that in a major clearing bank – or another large organisation, be it from the manufacturing, distribution or service sectors – your career will be managed centrally. Your career development is important to the organisation. You will be seen regularly to check up on your progress. You will be encouraged to sit examinations for the relevant professional body, and to gain independent, professional qualifications. You will be taught 'leadership', you will be taken on physical fitness courses, have your 'interpersonal skills' brushed up. You will stretched and stretched and stretched . . . and it is all in a good cause. In a nutshell, it all increases your 'added-value' to the organisation you are working for, and to you in your working life. You will be in a position to know more, to earn more, to operate at higher levels and to climb to the top. Indeed, these programmes really provide you with a map to guide you to the top. They should be seen in this light.

Enlightened managements recognise that many of their talented graduate and non-graduate intake will, in the fullness of time, leave that organisation for another. Frequently, they leave the sector altogether. Managements of major organisations are relaxed about this. They believe that their programmes have helped to stretch that individual to a greater realisation of their own potential, and that the person concerned will be a better and more worthwhile citizen as a result. These management development programmes cost the organisations concerned a lot of money. They see it as investment in the future, both for their organisations, and for others, if the person concerned decides to leave for pastures new. Credit given for such enlightened attitudes from major organisations is often scant and grudging, both from the persons concerned and in the wider context. This is a pity.

Opportunities

It is important both to spot and to grab opportunities. As Vincent Duggleby says, 'It is vital to seize opportunities'. But to be able to seize an opportunity you must be able to recognise it. Some people have the ability to spot opportunities, others haven't. Have you?

Think of an opportunity as a door which opens. You don't know what is on the other side. But you could be intrigued to find out. The next time you are talking about prospects for the future, just keep an ear open for what could be a hint of that opening door. Once you have the knack it is simple to develop.

The truth is that opportunities are there, for all of us, a lot of the time. It is sad if we pass them by just because we haven't recognised the door which opens and taken the chance to look through it!

The importance of competence

In the 1990s the key word with regard to work will be 'competence'. It is already identified as significant. Today training programmes from areas as diverse as financial services to retailing are focusing more directly on the field of competence. In a recent report to the Securities and Investments Board (the chief regulator of financial services in the UK), Dr Oonagh McDonald reviewed the need for professional training in financial services regulated under the Financial Services Act. She underlined the need for professional qualifications, and for training to be undertaken by the industry, to deliver competent professionals, equipped to handle their important relationship with the consumer buying their financial products and/or services.

You may well ask, 'But surely competence has always been significant. Who would employ someone who wasn't competent?' The answer is, alas, that very often there is a fair degree of wishful thinking involved, on both sides. The subject of competence in the past was more based on assumptions, and not in specifically checking out whether the person was or was not competent to handle the job in question. Even in the management of pension funds, much in the news over the past few months, those responsible for the management of this key and sensitive area have not been tested as to the level of competence they bring to their important duties!

So what is competence?

Dr Oonagh McDonald has defined it as, 'A quality of service which is achieved through the successful interplay of a number of attributes, practices and arrangements'.

Put in its most simple and concise form, to be competent is to be properly qualified for the job in hand. It means that the levels of skill, care and diligence, maturity of thinking, and judgement, are adequate to perform the function, whether this is in doing or in advising. It implies that the delivery of the function will satisfy the person or organisation commissioning it.

The reason that competence as a subject has come forward to the front burner is the late realisation of these facts. Although, as a group, managers are committed to improving the climate and effectiveness of their organisations, and they are very well informed about management, it would seem that they know little about themselves as managers. Admittedly, they know a very great deal about the functions involved in their work. They know how to organise, budget, control and so on. But there seems to be little or no consensus within or across organisations about the skills or characteristics which relate to superior organisational performance. Managers appear to have little awareness of their own strengths or limitations, or of the major contributions they bring to their organisations. In addition, it would appear that they know less than they should about what skills they need to develop in order to improve the performance of their work groups.

If you consider the revolutionary changes in the external environments, and the rapidly increasing rate of change on all fronts, you will readily recognise that revolutionary change is equally demanded in the way we structure organisations, and our jobs, in the overall culture.

So how do you rate in the competence stakes?

In order to answer this question you should address your characteristics as an individual. These will have emerged out of your general education and other forms of background and social life. They are the abilities and skills which you will be bringing to the organisation you wish to join. Your management will have to assess whether the values you bring are in conflict with their culture, or if they complement it. They will need to understand just what needs to be added to ensure that your contribution to the organisation is positive and at the level they seek. Answer the questions below to find out where you stand.

Knowledge

Do you have a good basic general knowledge?

Yes No

Do you have special knowledge in specialist areas? If so, identify.

Abilities

Do you have good general abilities?

Do you have abilities in certain areas? If so, identify.

Yes No

Do you have special skills? If so, identify.

Motivation

Would you say that you are highly motivated?

Do you like taking initiatives?

Have you achieved things by taking initiatives? If so, identify.

Values

Identify what you value:

Quality of life?

Money?

Status?

Reputation?

Now let us look at the subject of skills. Look at the categories below to give you an idea of where you stand (mark yourself from 1 to 10).

1 – 10

Language skills – verbal ability, written ability.

Numerical skills – number manipulation, quantitative procedures.

Communication skills – interpersonal skills, the ability to share ideas and understand the ideas of others.

If you have worked out where you stand from the use of the above checklists, you should have some idea about what you have to offer and where your talents really lie. Hopefully, you have listed your knowledge and abilities and have come to terms with an honest appraisal of how motivated you are. A clear indication of the values you hold will also help to steer you to where you want to end up, while the marks you have given yourself on your skills may be enlightening, to say the least! The pieces of the jigsaw should be starting to fall into place. Now, let us look at how you can build on what you have to offer, and in which areas.

Basic skills

Before you can assess your skills you need to know what they are. A skill is an ability to do something, but not being excellent at doing something does not mean that you have no skill at it! So what are these skills and how can you assess your skill in each area?

The basic skills are:

Planning skills – Focusing on the future, without being emotionally diverted by too much in the way of hopes or fears. The planning skills relate to gathering information, having ideas, diagnosing and analysing, predicting, anticipating, assessing and interpreting information. Use this as a list and mark yourself as to your ability on a 1–10 frame.

Doing skills – How to make things happen. Doing skills relate to using dexterity, co-ordination, motivating others, initiating, using enthusiasm, skill with numbers and communications (the use of language – reading, writing, speaking), using visual awareness, any technical skills you have, decision making, giving and taking instructions, prioritising, time management, negotiation, organising resources. Here again, use this as a list and mark yourself as to your ability on a 1–10 frame.

Consolidation skills – Sustaining the momentum, progressing the matters in hand, encouraging yourself and others, development of words, music, etc., using your intuition, attending to detail, speeding up, slowing down, listening, laughing, having fun. Use this list and mark yourself on a 1–10 frame.

Evaluation skills – Helping the learning process, to make decisions, to plan and perform better next time. The evaluation skills include assessment, the measurement of results, observing, seeing the bigger picture, being objective, drawing conclusions, decision making. Again, use the list and mark yourself on a 1–10 frame.

Working with the above lists, you should be able to draw some broad conclusions as to whether your position on skills is better or worse than you thought. Now you should take the trouble to check the matter out with a friend (or two or three). They may have formed a very different impression and, if so, you should know why they see you differently.

Basic competences

The basic competences are defined by the knowledge and skills needed to perform the jobs or functions required. They include the personal effectiveness skills which are more related to the individual project or task. So what are these basic competences?

Competence at planning – The ability to understand and use systems. The ability to understand generally, from legal and political environments to the strategic features of the organisation, also the more pedestrian and narrowly focused issues and areas.

Competence at organising – Organisation structure, job design, selection promotion, salary administration and all detailed organisational tasks, controlling these and co-ordinating them.

Competence at controlling – Systems for controlling operations at the specific level, including the ability to deliver quality in performance.

Competence at development – Measurement and evaluation of performance at the levels required, discipline, appraisal of individual performance.

Competence at interaction – Leadership, giving directions re roles, duties, rules, procedures etc., getting feedback and giving support.

If you intend to climb to the top you must ensure that you can understand and perform all these basic tasks competently. If you can't, you will be running the risk of being associated with negative organisational performance.

You will find this important subject of competence addressed in more detail in Part 3 Appendix 4.

Criteria for promotion

Here again, managements agree on the key criteria for the success of an individual, qualities which rate him or her for promotion. These are:

- enthusiasm for the job;
- willingness to learn from mistakes;
- evidence of motivation;
- at appraisal, ability to appreciate what is needed in order to develop further.

In addition, in today's conditions, social mobility is valued. Also rated are continuing education and interest in this, and ambition.

How to choose your type of organisation

It is important to know how to choose the right type of organisation to work in. You will have your own ideas about the area in which you would like to work. What you need now to determine is what 'type' of organisation is 'your type' of organisation. Here is a simple snapshot to help you to identify the different types:

The 'traditional' organisation – a little bit old-fashioned, with a clear structure – from the top to the bottom. In this type of organisation you will be paid to do a job of work but, perhaps, you won't find it too easy to get things changed.

The 'new-style' organisation – large, progressive, highly

73

motivated, where financial success is the be-all and end-all. In this type of organisation you will be worked hard, but the rewards should be good − if you can stand the pace.

The 'family-style' organisation − which may or may not be a family business. In this type of organisation the style is paternalistic. You may like this style of management or you may find it stifling. You will generally find that this type of organisation is more 'caring' than many others.

The 'entrepreneurial-style' organisation − where the thing you did yesterday is out of style and 'old-hat' today. This will stretch your mental − and physical − muscles. You may find working for such an organisation an exhausting experience, unless you are naturally inclined to being able to balance on the high wire!

How to identify a well-run organisation

What will be very important is to know that you have chosen to work in a well-run organisation. As you study the range of organisations you are interested to work in, how can you tell if it is well run or not? Here is a useful checklist. It relates to the human aspects which the balance sheet won't reveal!

- Do those who work there take care of the premises? Are the washrooms clean? Any vans and lorries in good repair? Are factory, offices or studios tidy? If employees 'care' for the firm's property it should be a good place to work in.

- Is conspicious corporate extravagance apparent in the reception areas? Do areas you may be called on to work in reflect mean and tight-fisted attitudes by comparison? If the difference is extreme, it frequently means that the management is too extravagant on things which don't matter fundamentally.

- Do those you see when you go in for interviews seem cheerful and lively? Are they helpful to you? If their attitude is positive it could be a good place to work in.

- Do those speaking to you, and interviewing you, know the

first names of the people they have working for them? Do you know whether the managing director spends his working hours on the company's business, or is he often away on the golf course, on charity and other external committee work, or on corporate entertaining? Can you find out? Good management is interested in those working for it, and very mindful of the need to put the company's business first at all times.

● Is there an employee share ownership plan? If so, this is good.

● Can the manager interviewing you explain to you what the company does in thirty words? He should be able to do this if the firm has a clear strategy and knows where it is going.

Your CV

Your CV is, of course, your key document in terms of achieving a job interview, or presenting yourself for a project or assignment in which you are interested. How it is presented and what it contains, is therefore of maximum importance.

Much has been written about what should and should not be in a CV. Here are some tips which you should find useful.

DO ensure that your CV is well laid out and typed accurately, containing no spelling mistakes etc.

DO ensure that it is factual, and not misleading.

DO ensure that you have studied some other CVs and know what they should and should not contain.

DO ensure that it contains:
   date of birth;
   education;
   any qualifications;
   details of jobs held and/or work done;
   information on achievements of note;
   whether or not you have a driving licence/car;
   information on wider interests, and/or hobbies;
   information on any clubs or groups you belong to.

In Part 3, Appendix 5 you will find a sample CV set out and explained.

Making the most of an interview

The matter of interviewing well is thought to be very complex by many. It is not. Some simple, applied common sense will help you to make the most of your opportunities at interview. Just think about it.

The priority for the person interviewing you is to ensure that, in the given time (usually thirty to sixty minutes) he or she gets a good and accurate 'snapshot' of you and your possible contribution to the post which is to be filled. It follows that:

- In the thirty-second time-slot which begins when you enter the room, you must give the best impression you can from your appearance. This short time-slot is most important. It forms the immediate impression, provides the outline which will be filled in during the interview. So ensure that your appearance 'fits' with the impression you want to convey. See Steps 7 and 9 for more information on this point.

- During the interview, you will be expected to convey accurately what you have done, what qualities and skills you have, what you can contribute to the organisation and why it is you rather than someone else who should be asked to fill the vacancy in question.

- During the interview, too, you should endeavour to give an impression of yourself in the wider sense, what sort of person you are, how willing you are to learn, how easy you find it to get on with people, how motivated you are and why this opportunity is the one you especially want.

- Most important, you must allow the person interviewing you time to talk about the organisation, about the job, about what is expected of you. You must question relevantly and observantly.

- It is also important to recognise just how nervous you are at interview time, and to resist the temptation to hide you nervousness under bluster, enthusiasm or verbosity.

Choosing between offers

In today's world you will be lucky to have to choose between job offers. However, it is possible because talented people are much sought after. In doing so, what are the factors to remember?

First, remember that choosing between two good options is always difficult. This is because the pros and the cons are generally very equally weighted.

Next, remember that it is important to take the long-term view, even though the reality is that you may not be in that job for many years.

Third, take your own personal considerations seriously. If there are factors which you can recognise that irritate you before you join the organisation, it is very likely that they will prove to be frustrating when you are working there in a day-in day-out capacity.

Fourth, remember that money is only one of many measures to take into consideration. Look through your own objectives etc., and see how well they match with what the particular jobs have to offer.

Finally, take the 'people' factor into consideration. You are likely to be happier and more fulfilled, and turning in a better contribution, if you like the people you will be working with and for.

Changing Direction

You may have decided that you need to change direction in your career. You need to inform the organisation you are working in that you will be leaving. How do you go about this in the best way? Here are some tips which should be useful.

DO keep the matter of leaving to yourself – don't gossip about it so that it is common knowledge in the firm's canteen or rest rooms.

DO ensure that the first person who knows about your intention to leave is your immediate superior. Do it formally. Make an appointment.

DO study what you intend to say about your reasons. Play down those which will be unpopular to the ears of the organisation. Play up the opportunities which you are seeking from a change in direction or a new job.

DO remember that it is human nature to feel a degree of 'rejection' when your boss knows a member of the team is leaving. In the words of one distinguished American businessperson, when asked about his response to the resignation of an executive – 'Quite simply, I accept it to his or her face. But my reaction is always the same – when asked about the person I say "Who? What is the name? Spell it."' This is harsh, but realistic. So bear this comment in mind when you are announcing your resignation, and put some sugar on the pill before you ask your boss to swallow it!

DO – even after you have made your news known – resist the urge to gossip about it to all and sundry! This is difficult, but it is very good advice.

DO avoid, at all costs, threatening your boss with a resignation in order to secure a promotion or salary increase. This policy really never pays off in the long term, even if it may appear to do so in the short term!

Vincent Duggleby has some wise advice in relation to judging the time to change direction or to get out. He says, 'Each profession has different age spans to which "being at the top" applies and within the profession there may be different strands. Thus an active reporter may be "at the top" in his or her twenties and thirties. By the fifties they are trading much more on knowledge and experience, and while writers can go on to any age, the pressure from those below is always there. I doubt whether I would fight to retain a place at the top beyond age sixty!'

Redundancy

Most people facing a possible redundancy will be older, with children beginning to grow up and the house nearly paid for. The position with regard to redundancy is governed by law. It provides for payment according to length of service, with some tax breaks to relieve the anxiety and pain which an unexpected redundancy causes the person concerned, and also his or her family and colleagues at work. But what options are available to provide help?

Most enlightened employers today make efforts to 'cushion' the redundancy blow. They do this in several ways:

- in-house counselling services;
- the employment of 'out placement' agencies, for counselling purposes and help in preparation of CVs and introductions to new job opportunities;
- the financing of 'out placement' courses for those who are being made redundant, to help them to plan their future;
- the financing of professional help with regard to checking up on the likely financial position and resources of the individual.

Looking on the bright side

It is important to ensure that you are looking for the possible advantages in redundancy. It can be seen as a new opportunity, for a new beginning. Many people have found that there *is* a bright side to it. For example, many interesting and successful new businesses have been spawned as a result of the redundancy of talented businessmen and women. Also, there are instances of wonderful new craftwork and paintings being executed by redundant executives, now with the time to indulge in their long-term hobbies and keen to exhibit their artistry. So don't look at redundancy as a bleak, black prospect. Find out what you have to offer. This checklist, hopefully, will help.

- Do you have a hobby? Can you develop it? Is it marketable? Can you make it so?
- Do you have a skill which you can use to good effect?
- Have you an urge to set up your own business? To work in a special area (for example with food – to run a pub or small country hotel? Or, with an informed interest in art, to start up a gallery?)
- Can you join with others in a similar position to discuss and develop ideas which can in due course be translated into firm

79

plans for a new business or professional initiative?
- Is there potential in your home to develop a business opportunity? Could your family help?
- Do you want, really want, to have a second or a third career?

The answers to these questions should signpost you as to your best way forward.

Retirement

Today, more than ever, retirement is considered as not being compulsory at a particular age. Indeed 'ageism' and discrimination against 'mature' applicants for jobs has been and is being discussed at Westminster against possible legislation being enacted to prevent this practice. It is none the less true that those approaching retirement age can find themselves gently (and sometimes not-so-gently) shuffled through the 'front door' of their organisations. In the main, enlightened employers either run pre-retirement courses themselves for their soon-to-be-retired employees, or they pay for those employees to attend such courses. Frequently, too, they enable - and pay for - personal counselling on the individual's financial resources against potential need. As time goes by these, and the available redundancy facilities, will be extended to demonstrate the 'good corporate citizenship' of the employing organisation.

Looking on the bright side

There is very definitely a bright side to retirement - provided that you have made prudent plans for it. But even if you haven't, a bright side can still be created.

The idea that people have passed their 'sell-by' date in their fifties and sixties is increasingly being discarded. And as I have said elsewhere in this book, it is possible that the law may intervene to ensure that formal retirement ages are dropped. If this is the case, you would be able to work, and earn an income, for as long as you wanted to. Indeed, you can make this ideal come true even now. Frequently, people have the urge to continue working but don't know how to set about it.

The fact is that the present waste of human experience and judgement is enormous, and a very important issue. The person who is retired from one activity, job or profession is rich in maturity – with experience and skills honed to excellence over the years. The retired are able to use their skills and to transfer them to others – for example, as teachers and motivators. They have much to offer to society. Frequently, however, it is the person himself or herself who, when 'retired', is reluctant to participate, who somehow feels a 'pariah', 'useless', 'discarded'. As a result, that person becomes virtually 'invisible'. People trying to find that particular mix of skills and experience cannot find them, cannot reach out to him or her.

The answer lies in your own hands if you are in the position of facing retirement. Be positive and consider that this is a 'new beginning'. It will enable you to add many new experiences, find new friends, grasp new opportunities and face up to new challenges – provided that your eyes are open and you can recognise them. The opportunities and challenges will be there, but it is up to you to ensure that your attitude can be positive enough to enable you to spot and make the most of the ones which come your way.

There are many, many people who, today, will tell you that the third age – the age of retirement – can be the happiest and most rewarding of all. It is really up to you as to whether or not you add to their number.

Remember

- 'Getting in' could be simpler than you think, if you know what you have to offer a large – or small – organisation, and you know, too, what they are looking for.

- Studying your own competences; knowing what they are, and how to develop them could be very valuable to you.

- If you are seeking to 'get in' on a work path in a less traditional setting, applying lessons from the traditional, and adapting them as necessary, could help your chances of long-term success.

STEP 4

——▲——

GETTING ON

In steps 1 and 2 you have come to know yourself, and to set your goals. In step 3 you have been advised on steps to help you to 'get in' the organisation of your choice.

You are now interested in making the best of the position you find yourself in. Areas covered in this step include advice on understanding management: company politics; how to get the information you need; and information on the way organisations judge the performance of those who work for them. Additionally, the roles of peer groups and mentors are discussed, as well as the key areas of training and self-development.

Now you really have your feet under the table, in your job, in your chosen career, in one of the professions, art, literature, the sciences or business. You've tested the water and you like it. You've realised that success isn't final, even though – when you begin – you think it is. The really hard part is staying there. So, you want to stay and to make progress in your particular field. How do you set about it?

There are many factors for you to consider. One such factor is that it is useful to be able to identify who may be important to you and why. You should also reflect on what you may be able to contribute to that person's career progression, as well as what he or she could offer you. It needs to be considered.

It is as well, too, to understand the company or establishment 'politics' and to recognise who is in the 'inside track' and who very definitely is not ... Getting to understand the organisation's 'culture' is most important. Try to find out what this is, when it first took root, how it developed.

A further factor is the information you need which will be useful so that you are able to identify your particular tool kit in relation to success. For example, if you write well, that is a skill which you should hone to perfection, using it to your benefit where you can. If you are good at analysis and presenting a case, here again is a tool you can use.

If you are weak in particular areas, say public speaking, then it is as well to recognise this fact and do something about it. Whatever you do, don't make the mistake of thinking public speaking isn't relevant to you. Each and every one of us has to make use of the technique to get our message across. It could be that the occasion is a small, informal gathering of only six people, or it could be a major public platform with hundreds present. The need is the same in each case. It matters a great deal. You need to know how to present your case, whether or not to use humour as a tool, to recognise and identify the reactions you wish to elicit from your audience and to decide how you are going to reach them. It is important also for you to remember very clearly that the message as you convey it may not be the message as your large or small audience may receive or interpret it! This is a simple fact, often forgotten even by the great and the good in the land, perhaps particularly by those from the political fraternity!

A further key factor is the recognition that you have two relationships at work – one is the professional relationship, how well you do the job. The other is the personal relationship, how you relate to people. This is very important and is too often given a low priority. Also, to get on, quite simply, you need to be noticed. Just look around you and take note of the popular 'live wire' – there always is one in any group. The chances are – when promotion is in the air – the person who has already made him or herself noticed will be considered. Don't, therefore, dismiss the idea that being popular isn't important. It can certainly help.

Being recognised and being seen to be a 'good egg' is not corny . . . It is useful and can provide a major capital asset and stepping-stone on your path to the top.

The Key Components

The importance of 'a light touch'

Remember, many points of importance are difficult to get over, because they represent critical views or judgements of the efforts of others. Remember, too, there are acceptable ways you can use to get your messages across. One of the most successful of these is if you are able to use humour as a tool. There are many people today in public life who do just this. No one ever resents a word they say because they get their points over with kindness, courtesy and wit. But do recognise whether or not you can use humour. Some people just can't, and if this is the case for you, please don't try! Humour is like a stiletto – it is fine and sharp . . . you could find yourself cut to pieces if you are trying to get your point across with humour, and you simply don't have the deft touch necessary to do it.

Think about those people you know and like to be with. They are fun. Everyone responds to them. When they enter a room it is as if a light had been switched on. Their style is pure champagne – and their substance is pure gold. The person who has that distinctive 'light touch' is much valued, and much loved. After all, we are all surrounded much of the time by the 'doubting Thomas's', and the gloomy and depressed. Is it not natural that we like to be with people who cheer us up? Very naturally we respond better to people whose presence reminds us that all is not desperately gloomy, that there is still much which can be achieved by a single human being.

'Given that everything else is equal, people like being with and doing business with people they like and get on with.' This is a point made often by the Baroness Phillips of Fulham. There is nothing sinister about this. It is pure common sense. But then common sense is perhaps not as common these days as it should be!

Getting on – the simple facts

Of course, we all like to get on. In a sense this is important for two reasons: the first is the recognition that you are doing a good job and the second is the satisfaction to yourself that this has been recognised. So how does a large organisation recognise the right person to promote, the person who is doing a good job? Sir Jules Thorn, one of the most successful post-war industrialists, a shy and modest young Jewish man who fled from Hitler's Germany with literally nothing to his name, on being questioned on how to get to the top identified it thus, 'It's very simple really – you just do the job you're paid to do 10 per cent better than they expect'. In discussion with many senior industrialists it would appear that the techniques to avoid are the ones which many believe to be correct and practical – writing a long-winded report on how you would reorganise the department; setting up an anti-establishment clique of your mates; telling your boss time and again that you think he or she is making a mistake, and this is how you would handle that tricky situation. It makes very sound sense.

But – if you are one of the bright, young people emerging from school, college or university – you will want to know how your peers, also representing bright, young, aspiring chief executives, are doing it – and how the example of how they are getting on and achieving progress in their chosen careers can be useful to you. You need to study their priorities and good advice which you can use and adapt to suit your particular needs. Read the case histories of the successful young business people featured in Step 10 of this book. Their careers to date, including their advice to you, the reader, contain a wealth of information and useful tips for you to follow.

Understanding management

It is, of course, important to understand how management works. While managements differ in style, nature of activity and focus, the priniciples which motivate them remain the same. At the simplest level, these are:

- to set management objectives;
- to agree a strategy to meet these objectives;

 - to agree a 'mission statement' encapsulating both the objectives and the strategy;
 - to set the appropriate plans for marketing, production, distribution, finance and general management;
 - to inform all the organisation's stakeholders (as appropriate, from shareholders to employees, from financiers to the local community and customers at all levels) of the principles, quality, production and other standards, by which the organisation stands.

The total of the above should encapsulate the 'culture' of the organisation.

There is a research technique involved in a number of management studies which you could adapt to give you a simple idea of the nature – and culture – of the organisation. Here it is. Just imagine that the organisation is a 'person'. Ask yourself these questions.

Is the person male or female?
Is the person young or old?
Traditional or unconventional?
Strait-laced or extrovert?
Has the person achieved much in the past?
What was the nature of the achievements?
Have there been failures? In which directions?
Is the person trustworthy?
Is the person fair? Generous? Tight-fisted?

and, finally, and most important –

What values does the person have?

If you consider your answers to these questions, and discuss them with other colleagues to check that your opinions are shared with them, then you will have a better idea of the organisation for which you are working. This should, in turn, help you to progress within it.

It is essential to ensure that you get as much information as possible in relation to objectives, strategy and operations, so that you can 'fit' yourself into the organisation's overall plan. In this way you will be helping yourself and should benefit in the long run. Gone are the days when a 'worker' was expected only to focus on the 'widget' whch he or she was making on the factory floor. Today's enlightened managements respond to curiosity, interest and enthusiasm expressed to them in the right way by those working in the enterprise. Such qualities demonstrate commitment; a benefit to management sought from all levels of employees.

Management Tiers and Procedures

Again, management structures differ from organisation to organisation. Identifying who is useful and can help you depends on knowing how your particular organisation is structured.

Here is an example, typical of large, manufacturing organisations.

The board of directors

At the very top, of course, is the board of directors. Typically this will be comprised of the 'executive' directors, the function heads. There will be a director in charge of production, a director in charge of sales and marketing, a personnel director, a finance director. Other directors may cover specialist areas of the organisation. The managing director is the 'boss'. Frequently he doubles this function with that of chairman, becoming in fact the chief executive (or CEO). This practice is increasingly being frowned on and, among the 'great and the good', there is growing support for the two jobs of chairman and chief executive (or managing director) being handled by two separate people. In addition, there are what are called the 'NEDs' – the non-executive directors. These are drawn from the ranks of the 'great and the good' and appointed by the executive directors of the organisation. Here again, change is on the way. The NEDs very frequently have another business connection with the organisation. They could be suppliers, the merchant bank or a friendly solicitor. It is thought that some 80 per cent of NEDs are involved with other business with the company. This is not good enough. Change being contemplated should ensure that the NEDs (who, incidentally, share the same legal responsibilities as executive directors, but may only have access to 5 or 10 per cent of the key information by comparison) are seen as properly 'independent' directors, not employed just to 'massage the chairman's ego' as too frequently is the case at present. They should be there, appointed by other stakeholders in the enterprise (employees, institutional shareholders, customers etc.) to be the custodians of their interests in the enterprise.

Today, being a member of a board of directors is more onerous than it used to be – and quite properly so.

The business of the board is to ensure that the company is meeting its objectives. It sets targets and monitors progress towards them.

Management committees

Reporting to the board at regular intervals will be a series of management committees. Their nature will vary from organisation to organisation. They will cover the whole spread of activities and every interest group, from employees, to factory, to sales and marketing, to distribution and fleet matters, to promotion, advertising, public relations, external relations, involvement with industry and government affairs, international bodies and so on. Those involved with the business of management committees will be the organisation's 'managers'. This relates to executives with what is called 'line' responsibility.

Decisions taken by the board are passed down the 'line' to the managers for implementation. It follows that each manager has to ensure that he or she knows those reporting to them. It follows, too, that they must have a clear idea as to the individual's capabilities, where their talents lie, where their interests focus and the level of their commitment to the organisation's cause. Management development matters should have a high priority in the management committees.

Company politics

Every organisation gets involved in company politics. The level of this can vary. In some organisations the 'in-fighting' can be horrendous as the ambitious struggle for power. Whether or not you wish to involve yourself in company politics is a decision for you. And whether or not you are involved, you will still need to know that you are getting on the inside track. How you do this, and the extent to which you get involved is again a matter for you.

How do you deal with office politics? Such things are very difficult to avoid. Can you turn them to your advantage?

If you want to avoid office politics you will probably have to be blunt and say so to someone who is persistently trying to persuade you to play a part. Making it known that you are a 'private' person can help. Also, you can play up your other out-of-office interests, but to someone who is really determined, perhaps the best route is to indicate that this really is not an area which interests you and you would prefer to side-step it.

On the other hand, if you are a person who is political – with a small 'p' – playing a part in office politics can be fun ... you may like, as many do, to 'have a stir'! Playing a part in office politics can definitely be advantageous – if you know what you are doing. Here again, the best and safest course is to recognise what your talents may be, and indeed if you do have any talents in this direction. If you honestly think you haven't, then unquestionably the wisest course is to avoid office politics. That often quoted cliché, 'If you don't like the heat stay out of the kitchen', is very true and sound advice.

The case histories in this book will give you examples of how the matter was viewed by those who are succeeded in 'getting on' in their different organisations.

Getting the Information You Need

The tools for success are information, and yet more information. So how do you ensure that you are 'plugged in' on the information grapevine?

Here again, the answer lies in effective 'networking'. This matter is dealt with in more detail under step 6 in this book. The checklist which follows should give you some help in accessing information.

- Ensure you are on as many distribution lists as possible, for organisation information which interests you.

- Ensure you get your organisation's newspaper or magazine and read it carefully. Comment where you can, either verbally or in writing.

- Get the firm's annual report and study this. Ask questions of the relevant executives in the organisation, in relation to points you may wish to raise.

- Join any groups which may be of interest. Contribute to them positively.

- Ask questions, make suggestions.

- Demonstrate your commitment – in as many ways as you can.

- Offer to help, where you can, as a contributor to the firm's newspaper or magazine, as a member of the social club, on a piece of work your immediate boss may be undertaking.

- Above all, be 'visible'.

- Take your level of popularity seriously.

Going through the checklist above should enable you to see where you can add strength to your position and demonstrate your commitment so that this can be valued by others in the organisation.

Appraisal and training

Most organisations today have re-thought the matter of regular appraisal and training. These matters are now given much higher priority.

Perhaps one of the most significant and depressing thoughts, as we pass through the 1990s, is that one in three of Britain's working population has no qualifications and no training. This is a sobering thought to reflect on in terms of planning your future. If you want to get on, you simply must take seriously the need to ensure that you have the qualifications and training to make the progress you want to make.

If you are a woman you won't need reminding that you need to be specially careful to fight your corner. It is a fact that 43 per cent of Britain's workforce are women and currently 'grossly undervalued and under-developed' in their potential for the economy. They are concentrated in a narrow range of occupations and largely confined to jobs stereotyped for women. Admittedly the problem has been recognised and there are many pious initiatives aimed at advancing the appointment of women, and to recognising them as a key national resource. So you may find things easier tomorrow than they are today! Press for your place on government training schemes and other recognised training initiatives.

Prepare yourself

Recognise the importance of doing the right amount of preparatory work to equip yourself for the life you wish to lead in the future. It is timely, therefore, to take a look at the subject of appraisal.

The regular appraisal procedure is generally carried out at least once a year in a major organisation. Enlightened employers favour a procedure which allows maximum transparency between the employee and the manager appraising his or her performance. The appraisal form will be made available to the individual and he will be invited to fill it in and then review – generally at a later date – the manager's opinion. This may reflect minor or major differences in relation to the individual's perception.

The form will deal with the following general areas.

Qualifications – Information on which relevant qualifications in the work sector the individual possesses, subjects passed, any prizes awarded.

Educational levels completed – Information on GCSE, CSE, O and A level grades received, any university and other qualifications received or sought.

Languages – Information on fluency in foreign languages, identifying these.

Driving capability and ownership of vehicle – identifying its nature (car, motorbike etc.).

Outside interests – Information on clubs, societies etc., which the individual supports.

Information on past experience – Covering a ten-year period.

Information on internal and external courses attended.

Information on interest expressed in working in other departments or divisions of the organisation.

This will be followed by an analysis of skills with a score system so that the individual can fill in where they see they score. A marking key will help them to complete this task. A series of other questions elicits the individual's responses on matters which will affect their progress in the institution.

At the end of the day, the formula enables both manager and individual to see where their opinions are shared and where they differ. It is an invaluable exercise if viewed in the right light by the individual. A specimen of the type of form which is used frequently can be found in Part 2, Appendix 6.

Training is given a high priority within a major organisation, as can be seen from the areas covered on the appraisal form. Management development is one of the keys to successful operation in any organisation. It is generally made available to those who can be seen as interested in 'getting on' at any level. Training is also getting a high priority from Government these days. The opportunities for self-development, continuing education and training are further developed under Step 8 in this book.

The roles of peer groups and mentors

Opinions gleaned from your peer group can be very valuable. The generosity of most of those who have made it to the top can be great when they are asked to talk to, advise and/or help those who are still on their way up a ladder of achievement. It is important, though, to be selective when asking for such help and to ensure that you can put your case objectively and not abuse the member of the peer group in terms of the time required to deal with your request or because of the nature of it.

Finding the right person to be your 'mentor' is another valuable way of getting the help you may need when you need it. In some organisations they have a system of establishing a mentor to help an individual they believe has talent and commitment to the organisation. In the course of researching this book many distinguished people from all walks of life were frank in explaining that they had sought, and found, mentors who had gone out of their way to help them to achieve their potential.

So, if you need to find a mentor, where do you look and what qualities are you looking for?

The ideal mentor is someone you respect for his or her achievements, someone you know shares your point of view on a number of key issues. It is not necessary for you to agree with your mentor on everything, but you must respect that person's opinion. You must look up to them, know that they represent what you would like to achieve, that advice given to you by them will be listened to, and acted on.

Be realistic when you are thinking of a mentor – find someone who will have the time to discuss important matters with you, will respect your confidence, and has the interest and ability to guide you.

It may sound as if you are looking for and expecting the impossible! But, the simple fact is, if you look, you will find ...

The right mentor can help enormously in so many ways, including dealing with worries you may have, helping you to motivate others, helping you to create the 'gravitas' you may need to achieve your potential in the organisation of your choice.

Having a mentor whom you respect and trust can be useful to you in many ways which are complementary to the mentoring function. He or she can help to establish you as a 'networker'. Increasingly in the 1990s we will be reading of the importance of networking. Even today we can see the emergence of more useful networks where the like-minded link up to join a common cause on an issue of importance. This, in turn, often leads to the development of important links with peer groups and mentors.

An interesting example of what can happen through networking has been the emergence of the new Breakthrough organisation. This charity is concerned with the issue of breast cancer, mostly in women but increasingly apparent in men – on both sides of the Atlantic. The aim is to recruit 15,000 businesswomen and to raise £1,000 from each, through networking in their organisations. The money will be used to fund an imaginative and totally new concept in healthcare and research – housing in one complex the scientists working on the research which could lead to finding a cure for a disease which kills many thousands every year, and the doctors and nurses involved in treating the patients. When complete, the new centre in central London will be the largest of its kind in Europe. It is immediately apparent that this concept has great appeal and that the many thousands who will be involved in achieving its objectives will be establishing other links of interest and importance to them in their own lives at the same time.

Finally, here are three important pieces of advice. Jan Walsh, a pioneer in consumer affairs and a Manager at BT, says, 'I suppose my greatest difficulty has been to develop the art of listening – not just to what people say, but to their hidden agendas. This is a lesson I'm still learning and it's not easy for one as voluble as I! But it is good advice to become a good listener.'

From Elizabeth Nelson, a highly successful businesswoman. She comments, 'Probably in my early career having too much faith in managers I reported to was a difficulty I encountered. It took me ten years of my working life to realise that I wanted to be in charge of my own company, so recognise if this is true of you, too.'

From Roderick Dewe, who has achieved much in terms of international public relations consultancy and with many achievements in the world of financial PR and privatisations comes wise advice, although it may be difficult to achieve. He says, 'Never borrow money which you can't afford to repay back immediately if you have to.'

Remember

- 'Getting on' in your work probably depends more on the efforts you make than you think.

- It is important to look carefully at what your organisation is striving to achieve, and how well you can 'fit' with it.

- Management structures, systems and operations need to be understood, and you should try to respond positively to them.

- Finding the right role model or mentor could be invaluable.

Advice on getting on

Phil Kirkham, Senior Manager on Management Development at the National Westminster Bank plc, has this advice for the reader of this book.

TEN DO'S

1. Do set career objectives before applying for a job.

2. Do ensure that the company you approach can deliver those career objectives.

3. Do make sure that the skills the company is looking for match your own. Know yourself!

4. Do give the company time to deliver on career progression. Initial training is essential but can often be dull and not 'challenging'. Stick with it.

5. Do ensure you progress rapidly with any examination/ qualification that the company expects you to achieve. This is a sign of your commitment.

6. Do ensure that the personnel section of the company know you and know what you are looking for out of the job. It's your life to manage, not the company's.

7. Do be prepared to change track if you realise the job is not for you. Training costs money and it is better for both parties if early decisions are made where there is an obvious mismatch of skills.

8. Do ensure that your ambition is matched by the company's view of your potential. Marked differences will lead to frustration.

9. Do remember as you progress that one of the most important managerial functions is to help identify and develop potential in others.

10. Do be realistic and flexible. The aim of the company is to be successful and to make money, not to provide you with a perfect career path. Periods of economic recession or

organisational restructuring bring rapid change. Be positive and supportive during these periods, as the most positive indicator of managerial success is the ability to manage change.'

TEN DON'TS

1. Don't pretend to be something you are not. It is understandable to try to impress at interview but my best advice is – be yourself.

2. Don't assume that all companies are similar when it comes to training and development – they aren't. Ask sufficient questions to satisfy yourself on their policy.

3. Don't assume that career progression will be put on a plate for you – whatever accelerated entry scheme you join – promotion has to be earned.

4. Don't ignore the culture of the organisation. There are ways of getting things done. Everyone likes the individualist, but it is he or she running the company!

5. Don't press for jobs in areas where your skills are limited. Many good careers have ground to a halt where a high-profile job has been badly handled. Play to your strengths.

6. Don't ignore continuing education. Night-school, part-time business courses etc., can be useful. Change, including the management of change, is with us to stay. Be seen as up to date with management theory: it shows your commitment.

7. Don't put other people's ideas down as impracticable – just because you didn't think of it first. Evaluate, and if it's good, support.

8. Don't forget the people you work with. Not everyone comes to work for the same reason. Motivations are different, so don't impose your values on others.

9. Don't become destructive if your career does not progress as far as you want it. The company is a business trading for survival, and it does not need internal strife.

10. So you've made it to the top! Well done! Don't alienate the people who helped you to get there. You didn't do it all on your own. Don't lose their allegiance and respect or you might be taking the first steps down the slippery side of the slope.

STEP 5
▲

SELLING YOURSELF

The first steps on the ladder of success need all your time and effort.

This step follows logically when you have got time to breathe and review your next moves. What are the essentials? The step covers the key areas of the importance of ideas; it identifies the factors for success and how to make use of them; it discusses the importance of commitment to success and the importance of confidence.

By now you are established on your career path. You have absorbed the needs of the work you are involved in and have mastered your relationships with those around you. It is time to take a wider view. This step helps you take that wider perspective.

Having decided that you are striving for the top, it is valid at this stage to take a look at how good or bad you may be at 'selling' yourself.

It may not be an attractive proposition to consider that you are like a packet of detergent trying to find a buyer but, alas, there is always an element of this in life. It is as well to recognise it at the start.

The image of 'selling' as a career, as a task, as a skill, is not good in the UK. This is said with regret because, unfortunately, the low regard we have for selling has lost us much of value to the country.

Our markets have been eroded, and innovations made and developed in this country have been marketed and sold, profitably, from other countries as a result of poor marketing and selling here. Gifted young people (and those older), have too often been brought up in the belief that selling is the sort of 'trade' that 'gentlefolk' won't soil their hands with. This is a pity. Many opportunities have been missed as a result. Admittedly other areas, too, are regarded with as low – nay, even lower – esteem, in the political arena for example. But it is as well to recognise that everything, literally everything, in life has to be 'sold'. This remark may seem outrageous, but is it?

Let us look at some examples.

An idea has to be sold.

If you are making a special meal, you want it to be appreciated, and to elicit the right response from those eating it. The concept that it will be enjoyable as an experience has to be sold – by table, layout, lighting, the serving dishes you use and so on.

When you want to sell your car or your house, you don't let people see it at less than its best. You won't want them to look at it filthy, with damage apparent and generally in a decrepit condition. You may not go as far as some car dealers, with special leather smell sprayed on the upholstery, or some house sellers, who put a delicious lamb casserole into the oven to impress a likely buyer with its delectable aroma. But you do your best to show your prized asset in a decent light!

So, the idea of selling yourself isn't – in truth – so outrageous. In fact we are probably doing it all the time, but we don't recognise it properly.

One thing is certain – successful people take selling themselves, their concepts, their ideas, their beliefs very seriously indeed.

So, how do you set about it?

In this context there are three points to remember at all times.

The first is that nobody, absolutely nobody, *likes* 'a clever beggar'. So don't make the mistake of always appearing as a 'know it all', tempting as it may be, and relevant though the points you want to make may be at the time.

99

The second is that while points that you might make to get your message across are no doubt important, many of them will carry much more weight if they are delivered by others. So, goodwill and the favourable opinion and endorsements of others are important.

The third point is that it is essential − to sell successfully − to be able almost to 'get into the mindset' of the person you are wishing to sell to. You must know as much as possible about him or her, about their likely attitude and response to your proposition, about what they are *wanting* to hear. Whether you are dealing with the captains of industry, the 'great and the good' or your immediate superior at work, the point is equally valid. The capacity to be sensitive to the other person, the capacity to 'listen' and to distil from your proposition the items that will find an echo, a response in the mind of the receiver of your message, is essential before you can successfully sell yourself.

Remember what your final objective should be − to get others in your particular world of work, those who are already 'upstairs', to want you to join them.

The Key Components

The importance of ideas

From a very early age it is important to recognise the significance of ideas. The ability to have ideas and to try to make others see their relevance is stimulating. It opens doors in a way most other techniques don't. Recognise that to demonstrate that you have good, practical and workable ideas can *sell* you in a most desirable way, without making you appear overly 'pushy'! You are seen to be selling your ideas perhaps, not yourself.

Remember also the fact that very few people will reject, out of hand, the chance to discuss and consider a new idea − providing it is relevant and put to them in an interesting and objective way, preferably so that they can see it could help them.

Of course, there are many pitfalls to be wary of, many mistakes you could make. One of the most persistent mistakes made in this context is yielding to the temptation of putting up too many ideas when invited to walk through the door you have 'opened'!

Robert Heller, a very distinguished journalist and editor, founder editor of that authoritative business monthly, *Management Today*, expressed it thus, 'Never go to anyone with more than one idea. It is a complete switch off'. You may know he is right – but still find it difficult to take his advice.

Ideas can be sold, simply, without fuss, and with minimal expense – if you have the right idea, and can present it to the right person, and at the right time.

On this matter of introducing new concepts, of the many factors to be considered when trying to sell new ideas, getting the timing right is the most important.

When the timing is right even a concept which is less than perfect may find a willing listener, whether or not he or she is a potential buyer.

The importance of marketing yourself

Bear in mind that times are changing – fast. In the past selling has had a bad name, and perhaps it still clings. Its 'big brother', marketing, however, has a glossy, slick image and today many of the bright boys and girls wants to be in the business. What is the difference between the two?

Marketing is taking the wide view – deciding what you have to offer and what you wish to achieve. It is about objectives, strategy and tactics. It is also about planning, and ensuring that research has been done to confirm that the effort contemplated has a good chance of success. It is about deciding what tools you need, where you will get them, how you will use them. It is also about what it will cost, in terms of time, effort and money, and how long it will take to achieve the required results. And it is about the timing of the operation, and the monitoring of the short and long-term results.

Selling is the practical operation. It is about making the right approach to the 'target', in the right way and at the right time. It is about opening doors and walking through them, about seizing opportunities, about bringing new concepts to the attention of those who need to know about them. It is about convincing the customer. And it is about 'closing the deal'. This is often the hardest and least understood process. Many people know exactly what they want to achieve, make a good case for it, and then are concerned when they discover that their good idea has wandered off; that the concept they put in front of someone who received it with enthusiasm just hasn't 'gelled' – the deal has not been closed. What they need to be aware of is their responsibility to bring the deal (whatever it is about) to fruition. If you know clearly what it is that you wish to achieve, you are better equipped to achieve it.

In order to get what you want from your life and in your journey to the top, it is important first to ensure that you know or can learn how to market and sell yourself, and/or your ideas. As Peter Hayes says, 'I have consistently underestimated the necessity to market, that is to tell the world how good I am and how good my company is. This has always been anathema to me, as I was brought up not to blow my own trumpet, so I find it a hard thing to do – at least corporately. I do know it to be a mistake but it is one I still make. Incidentally, I think it is more of a mistake in this day and age than it was twenty years ago.'

The sentiments expressed by Peter Hayes are echoed by the Baroness Phillips, JP, who comments, wryly, 'Because of my Catholic background with the emphasis on humility, I have probably always undersold myself!'

Secondly, you must learn, too, how your reactions, attitudes and any emotional responses you may have, could hold you back.

The third, and perhaps most important factor, is that you should recognise what you may be doing which does hold you back, today: to know too what to do about it, and where to look for options to consider and action to take.

There is no magic formula – you need to apply a lot of basic common sense. After all, you are really seeking:

- to decide your messages and their targets;

- to reach those right people, and to convey the right messages to them;

- to understand what they will react to, and what they will react against;

- how to get them to accept what you have to offer.

So, what do you have to do?

This is both simple and straightforward. You must:

- identify your strengths, talents and interests;
- build your self-confidence;
- recognise how to sell yourself, and/or your ideas;
- do it.

Factors for Success – Make Use of them for Selling

We are living through constant changes – these can be seen as threats or opportunities. Much will depend on whether you are a negative person (seeing all the problems) or a positive person (stimulated by the excitement of the opportunities). It is not just bad to be the former and good to be the latter. Each has merit. What is important is to know with which you identify, and to balance both factors in your judgements.

Here are some factors to consider:

Are you flexible? If you are caught up in major *change* in your life or in your work, do you view this with alarm? Is your instinctive reaction to protest against the position, or do you welcome it as a chance to build on, an opportunity for improvement, for innovation?

Do you fear the unknown? You may be very comfortable in a given situation. You know what you are doing, and you know how to do it. You know that 'the process' has proved itself. If asked to do things differently, or to suggest a different way of doing things, how do you react? Because you may be stepping into the unknown, does this cause you problems? Does it cause you to react by trying to find all the reasons why the change should not be undertaken? Do you consider that such a reaction

103

could lead to loss of the opportunity to 'sell' your capabilities to those around you?

When faced with a problem, do you consider the overall implications? For example:
- Is the problem unique or can solutions be 'borrowed' (from experiences in other contexts)?
- Is the situation new to you?
- Is there a need to solve it? Or will the existing method of handling it work, perhaps with minor modification?
- How should it be handled then?
- What is the desirable solution? For the problem and for you personally?
- What are the likely outcomes? Good? Or bad?

Can you cope with change, stress or fear? This is not a frivolous question. Most people perhaps do not consider this matter sufficiently when the problem is not immediate. The 'fear' factor is important. You can find out whether you can cope with 'fear' by asking yourself these questions.

	Yes	No
Can you face giving up everything in the current status quo in order to take advantage of an opportunity for change for the better?		
Can you cope with threatened change for the worse?		
Do you believe that you are too set in your ways to contemplate a major change in direction?		
Do you believe others are forcing change on you for their own reasons, and are they good ones? For you?		
Do you believe that the effort just won't be worth it?		
Have you studied the consequences of your actions – in all categories, in relation to selling yourself?		

	Yes	No

Have you determined satisfactorily just exactly what you are selling?

If you have spent a little time considering the points raised above, you should have a clearer idea of how comfortably you would view any extra effort spent in selling yourself. It is important to be honest with yourself and recognise your basic attitude to selling. If you see it as a challenge, then if you focus on this area it should reap you real rewards. If you have problems with the concept of selling, then you should find colleagues who are good at it and discuss the matter openly with them. They may be able to help you to get over your reservations and provide you with practical tips on how to deal with the matter.

Your commitment to success

Are you committed to yourself and your success? This may sound like a very simple question to which you can easily answer 'Yes, of course!' But have you examined the evidence on which your answer rests?

This evidence can be easily assembled. Answer the questions given below and you will find out where you stand.

- Are you turning over a new leaf, or have you always been committed to yourself and your success?
- Have you made a good resolution like this one before in your life? Did you keep it? With what results?
- What past investment have you made to this commitment in yourself? In terms of time, money? How is this evidenced?

A glance at the position as it is today will give you the answers. Just look at your current pattern of behaviour and how you react and respond to others — at home and at work.

- Are you considered 'reliable'? When you make a commitment do you fulfil it? To others? To yourself?
- Do you read about success and successful people when possible?

– Do you spend any time examining your potential and self-development prospects and opportunities?

The answers to the above questions will give you a view as to whether you are as alert, motivated and committed as you should be if you are really striving for success in your sphere.

Positioning yourself for success

Success is really about winning at what you are attempting to do. So, how do you sell yourself to win? Remember that many of the features and attributes in someone you can identify as a winner are similar to those you can recognise in a first-class salesman or saleswoman. Your attitude, however, should not be that of many a 'star' in the sales team, the person who is really interested only in meeting his or her forecasts, or achieving the best bonus, or winning the promotion incentive of a fortnight's holiday in Bermuda! You should be guided by broader and wider principles which also relate to ethics and good citizenship. However, some of the techniques used successfully by salespersons could usefully serve you. Here are some tips which you can consider.

Most successful salespersons study the techniques of remembering names and faces. Try to improve on your current rating in this context.

Remember the importance of research. This does not refer to research in the accepted sense of the word. It relates to researching the background, special interests, quirks and other factors in those you are in contact with. Nothing impresses more than remembering an unusual hobby or the detail of a story told on a particular occasion. Successful salespersons study these carefully and use the information to best effect, on the right occasion. Do you give this area any thought? If not, you should consider it.

Think about the importance of contacts in the workplace. This is often a neglected area in terms of selling yourself in the wider context. But successful salespeople recognise that the workplace is central to getting the message across about what you, as an individual, are doing, and about what you hope to achieve in the future. It should, therefore, be an area to which you give attention.

Finally, it is as well to bear in mind that, in recognising the importance of selling yourself so that you can be recognised as a 'winner', you also achieve additional 'insurance' – because it is not easy for a winner to be turned around and identified as a 'loser'! This 'insurance' can be obtained in several ways. For example, if you have been successful in selling yourself, you should be known as a winner and so you are less likely to lose out and be fired than someone who is not – because you will have made many friends in your organisation and outside it. Your name will be alongside those of others who, when the chips are down and are even, the management will want to keep and not lose for morale and other goodwill reasons.

Planning for success

Every business – whether making, distributing and selling a product or a service – starts on the premiss of a business plan. This includes agreement on strategy and the development of a marketing plan. It is no less valid and useful for the individual.

So how do you set about it?

Your personal marketing plan should include a short, crystal-clear analysis of how you see yourself, where you are now and where you want to go. The individual mountains which you want to climb should be identified. As an example, answer the following questions.

Who am I? (Fill in a short description of yourself, maximum of 100 words.)

Where am I now? (Give a short note of your present position, age, background, current job or other activity.)

What do I have to offer? (Describe your talents, positive qualities and major attributes.)

What are my 'hang-ups'? (Give a frank list of problem areas in your personality together with lack of qualifications and other minus factors.)

Do I welcome change and can I accept it? (Answer this question – giving as much detail as you can on your attitude to change.)

Where do I want to be in five years' time? In ten years' time? (Give a clear and precise picture – even if it is ambitious. Dreams, after all, are there to be realised – where possible!)

Do I sell myself? (Answer this honestly.)

Do I find it easy to learn new methods, new techniques? (Again, this requires an honest answer.)

What do others think of me? (Make a list of people whose opinions you value and give an indication of what you think they think about you. Check it out if you can.)

Why should the 'buyer' of my concept, idea, service buy me? What advantage would it give him or her?

Answering these questions should help you determine your strengths and weaknesses in the marketing of 'You Limited'. (See Part 3 Appendix 8 for further details about this.)

Success outside work

It is important, too, to remember that success outside work can help to sell yourself inside work. Your achievements in other directions are of interest to those you work with and for. So it is important to identify those which are of consequence, and to find the right way to make them known to your colleagues at work and your managers. Natural curiosity means that we are interested in knowing more about our colleagues. This is something on which to build in your way to the top.

And look at the matter with a broad view – hobbies which are unusual and other related interests are also matters of curiosity to your colleagues and could help them to get a better 'snapshot' of who you are, what your interests are and the value you bring to the functions on which you are engaged.

Who can help?

The lists of people who can help you to achieve what you want from your life and from work is long indeed. It is as well, though, to remember that it is always easier to work with a few well-chosen people than to try to create a wide net of adherents. The right few can spread your influence more widely. Choosing those who can help you also means considering what you can do to help them. Help is always easier to obtain, and is better and more effective if it is a 'two-way' street.

The spheres of potential influence lie in a predictable number of directions. These are:

- those in your family;
- close personal friends and useful acquaintances;
- those in your circle of interests, hobbies, specialist interests, sports etc;
- professional advisers, from your doctor to your solicitor, accountant etc., but keep a wary eye out for any fees which they may need to charge you for advice on a professional level;
- colleagues at work;
- those in your 'peer' group.

In creating this list, be wary of including only those who agree with you. It is important, where possible, to include people of consequence, even if they don't immediately share all your opinions and concepts. It is also important to include people you respect and who could, arguably, be cleverer than you or are likely to be more successful. These are the people who will be in the position to 'bring something to your party'. You should also be aware of your responsibility to ensure that you, too, can 'bring something to their party'!

Action plan for 'You Limited'

Having looked at the above areas and filled in your answers to the questions, the next matter of importance in selling yourself is to draw up an action plan. Calling yourself 'You Limited' may help you to focus more objectively to this end. The following checklist should be helpful. Please fill in and/or delete, as applicable to your circumstances.

What I am wishing to sell is:
   an idea, a concept;
   myself, into a new job;
   myself, into a better job;
   WHY? BE CLEAR ABOUT YOUR REASONS

   what I have already achieved;
   what I should like to achieve, given the opportunity;
   something else (please identify).
   WHY? BE FRANK AS TO YOUR OBJECTIVES

Am I sufficiently prepared to set about my objectives?

Do I know where to turn for help and advice should I need it?

Do I know how to sell myself?

What is my time-scale?

When is my 'start date'? (The answer to this question should be 'Right now!')

In Part 3 Appendix 8 you will find the Action Plan for 'You Limited' set out. If you complete it, filling in the boxes provided, you should have your own personal Action Plan. You will then be able to work at implementing this in the way you think best.

Criteria for success

Finally, it is important to monitor and review the progress you may be making – also to set your criteria for success. The following structure of thinking about your objectives, aims and methods will at least serve to start you thinking about how you, as a person, fit into them.

My basic objective is . . . (State this.)

My time-scale to achieve the objective is . . . (State this.)

Monitoring – make a few headings and update these regularly, noting the progress you are making. Ideally, update every eight weeks. The headings could be:

enlarging my contacts – people I have met in the period who have something to offer in my plan of things;

getting my message across – opportunities seized in the period to put across a point of view, make a statement, create a discussion document of importance;

positive contributions I have made in the period to the plans/campaigns of others – list when, what, where;

mistakes I have made – list these too;

progress I have made – set up a points system and award yourself points on progress, deleting points for failures or mistakes.

Review progress, say quarterly. In this context try to include comments or opinions you may be able to glean from others. Make a positive effort to see yourself as others see you, which is not easy. It can be uncomfortable, as anyone will tell you who has had the experience of seeing themself in a reverse mirror – in other words, as we really are and not simply the 'mirror image' which is familiar and which we see in the looking glass every day.

The Importance of Confidence

And now for a final word – on the subject of confidence. Confidence is very important indeed in striving to reach the top, whatever mountain you are trying to climb. And the line between confidence and arrogance is a very fine but important one. The first is eminently desirable and the latter is to be avoided at all costs.

Confidence is, simply, having faith in yourself. It means that you know where you are going and what you are doing. It means that your manner is assured, that your attitude is direct, that you have done the necessary homework to believe that your views stand up to examination.

But it is very easy indeed for a confident person to go over the top, sliding across into attitudes which others may see as too bold, or as impudent, or as intrusive.

111

We have often read of the City that confidence is all-important. If there is confidence there the indices in the stockmarkets tend to stay steady and rise. If there is not confidence then free-fall can be a frightening experience, rapidly wiping billions of pounds off stock and share values – as has happened on more than one occasion over the past few years.

So ensure that you have done the background work in order to be confident as you sell yourself. You will hardly ever see a successful person who has not got confidence in themselves and what they are doing. But remember – real confidence requires internal honesty, usually based on striving and self-doubt.

Remember

- Selling yourself needs positive effort on your part.

- Selling yourself effectively requires a recognition of your basic objective and how you want to achieve it – over defined periods of time.

- Regular monitoring and ruthless – independent – appraisal of your successes and failures, are essential to success.

- Note that a few weeks of asking questions may well lead your own ideas to evolve. This will be useful and add realism to your efforts.

- Your effort should be very worthwhile in the long term, especially if you put the lessons you learned into practice.

STEP 6

▲

EARNING YOUR KEEP

This step is important all through your working life. However, it can be said to be more relevant as you are progressing onwards and upwards. At these stages competition is greater and there are fewer contestants seeking to achieve the leadership role.

This step offers guidance in the important areas of what organisations are looking for and current practice: it identifies the 'alienation factor'; offers an 'Earning your keep' checklist; and discusses networking in more detail.

'Earning your keep' will mean different things to different people. If you are trying to climb the business ladder it will mean consolidating your position in the organisation, building contacts to benefit you and your company, stimulating business ideas, making profitable progress and so on. In the wider context of work it will mean sharpening up your thoughts if you are an academic, striving yet harder to reach your idea of perfection if you are an artist, musician or, dare I say it, an author.

Earning your keep benefits you in the long run in many ways and should be viewed in the wider context of your life as a whole. For example, as Janet Brady puts it, 'To balance the commercial side I head up a charitable-based organisation. It has been going twenty-two years and represents the women in senior to junior management roles.'

In all contexts – wide or narrow – it will be the realisation that you should be operating in a wider context as time goes by; and that the requirement – from yourself and from others too – is for higher and higher standards of excellence in performance that is important, and the key to your motivation.

When you are known to be earning your keep in the narrow sense of your current job, you will find that you are offered other opportunities in the wider context of community, charity and to help on projects related to the key issues of the day. You will be polishing up your reputation as a person who 'makes things happen'.

This is what making the best use of human nature and potential requires.

We, all of us, are less than perfect. We know that as a fact. This makes many ask: why bother about making progress? But we do have an inbuilt mechanism which – in most of us – makes us strive to become better at what we do in some field or other, not necessarily work. Whether or not we recognise it, this human urge depends, in no small part, on the influences to which we have been exposed during our lives.

But making the effort to do well, and then better, is up to us, and is well worthwhile.

Until fairly recently the driving need to be profitable, or cost-effective as a person was less apparent. That is not to say that it didn't exist. It just seemed, say twenty years ago, that life was more comfortable and cosy than it is now. Jobs were more secure, and large organisations looked after their employees almost from the cradle to the grave. Firms were asking their talented staff to do more, and to take greater responsibility, and to become more 'front of the house'. Quite simply, the persons in question, those with ability and talent, had been noticed.

In this day and age, however, things are very different indeed. Today those wishing to climb the ladder of success need to be very mindful indeed of what is expected of them. There is much competition, but they also get a lot more help – other people identify to them how they will be judged and help them to develop their potential. To this extent they are luckier than earlier generations.

If you want to be truly successful in business (and in any other field for that matter) you need to be very single-minded about it. It leaves very little time for anything else. This is not to say that those who are climbing these particular mountains set out to be selfish or are less than generous as human beings. But it is a simple fact of life. Frequently it doesn't even relate to the amount of money they accumulate.

Setting out to be a captain of industry or a millionaire is quite simply the most fascinating thing in the world to those who seek to travel this path. They enjoy the 'buzz' it brings. Everything else comes a long way behind.

Frequently, however, it leads the striver to fairly unattractive behaviour. So much so that we become glad that we have avoided that risk!

One example of this is the very noticeable 'hoovering' exercise done by some of the ambitious. Every time, let us say at a reception or even a cocktail party – where they are present, they can be observed 'hoovering' up the assembled guests they do not know to ensure that they learn whether or not they could be interesting, important or useful in the future. It is amusing to note that they do not recognise that their techniques are noticed'!

There are other irritating traits of the ambitious and would-be successful too. When talking to you in a roomful of people, their eyes are everywhere else, noting and automatically filing the people they don't know yet and then, later and in due course, you see them circulating around the room checking out those they don't know who could be useful.

In another context it is said of some of the over-ambitious that 'he was one of those people who, in front of assembled company, would give you a cheque for your charitable cause and, later, when no one was looking would present you with a bill which was several times the size of the donation he had just made!'

These are all warning signs to note as suitable cautionary tales.

Perhaps the motto is 'if you are going to use this particular technique, don't be so obvious about it' or 'what are your real (as distinct from short-term) priorities?'

But 'earning your keep' also involves operating in the wider context. Networking, widening your horizons and recognising your responsibility to put something back into the society which has educated you, and enabled you to earn a living, is a responsibility to be reckoned with.

Most of us are tempted to be involved with many 'worthy' organisations. Sometimes we feel we have to run to ensure that we are not letting down the people who are paying our salaries!

There is also a temptation for people to play someone who is earnest, enthusiastic, well-meaning and hard-working, for a sucker! Many is the initiative which has foundered as a result of the lack of follow-through and motivation of others. Many ideas now 'belong' to others who find it 'convenient' to forget where and how they were originally spawned. However, comfort yourself – if this applies to you – with the thought that you can always think up new ideas to replace those that slipped away.

What is important, though, is to recognise that, by their very nature, human beings are often predators of other people's initiatives. To understand what may happen frequently, does not mean you can prevent it. What is important, however, is to recognise that the fundamental fact is that the idea may 'fly' and while that doesn't help to pay the rent, it does have some satisfaction for the author of the initiative . . .

A sobering thought is that no idea, no matter how brilliant it may be, is of any use at all by itself. It has to be 'sold', and then comes the most difficult part of all – it has to be made to work . . . And, finally, it has to deliver the result anticipated by its originator.

'Intellectual property' is the new jargon name currently in vogue and, hopefully soon, and not before time, protection will exist so that your bright, innovative ideas, do not get 'ripped off' by others as much in the future, as has been the practice in the past. There are, of course, 'formal' methods of protecting innovations in the forms of patents and trade marks, also by registered designs, copyrights etc. These all protect their sorts of specified intellectual property. They are, however, of little help to those engaged in 'concepts' and 'ideas', which are considered as more 'informal' aspects of intellectual property.

So, how do you earn your keep in an organisation? Here are some factors to consider.

Key Components

What organisations are looking for

It is important to recognise the different time-frames involved. At twenty-five most people have drive, and at least some creativity and originality. At thirty-five, in the main, they are working by the rule book. They have recognised that working by the rule book and not breaking the rules means they get rewarded, so it is not surprising that the fabulous ideas they once had are more difficult to find and bring to the surface.

But, providing the person behaves in the sense agreed by their immediate superiors at work, that is generally sufficient. Most people do have to recognise that they need to play the organisation system. If Joe Soap is taking over a job from Bill Bloggs who came in early and left late, then Joe Soap has to think hard and long before he immediately changes that system, coming in a minute before time and clocking off exactly on time! If he is wise he will settle in gently and change gradually so that others recognise and feel comfortable that he is playing by their rules. This is no more than sound common sense, but it is wise to recognise its value.

It is as well, therefore, to be sensitive as to what the organisation will be looking for if you are keen to climb the ladder in an established business. It is also important to recognise that your employers will be looking at different criteria in relation to your earning your keep at different times in your life.

How organisations deal with the 'awkward devil'

The 'red for danger' flags can certainly go up quickly if you are likely to be dubbed 'an awkward devil'. This is generally related to those who don't conform, or are touchy, difficult, volatile. It could simply be that it is a case of the square peg in the round hole. Today professional management is well experienced in recognising this and dealing with it appropriately by putting the person into a department better fitted for the use of their particular set of skills, experience and personality. It is rather more difficult to deal with the 'awkward'. So what are the options?

Identification is not the problem, but dealing with the problem is. In almost all cases enlightened senior managers tend to examine their behaviour or other relevant people's behaviour in terms of making the job more satisfying to that individual, regardless of the categorisation. In most cases, they may feel that such individuals may benefit from tasks performed within teams so that their team-building capabilities can be assessed. If there is little ability or desire to work in a team, then the genuinely creative person should be allowed to develop in a non-line position. Most, however, do want an audience and, given the opportunity, could work well in a team.

At most enlightened major employers, including NatWest, they believe that the accurate recruitment process results in the company being exposed to less risk from awkward characters. They believe that the assessment process picks up creativity, but that the manager needs to learn how to perform a job in a strategic area. 'Awkward' people may have a lot to contribute, and a spell in strategic planning may help those qualities to surface. This technique is often used to enable employers to better assess latent potential.

The alienation factor

In any step reviewing 'Earning your keep' it is as well to take a look at the negatives. Managements spend many hours of their time and large sums of money looking at the factors which alienate employees from their organisations. They study what they can do about these. So what are these alienation factors?

First, it is best to look at the basic forces of society and how they are moving. In very general terms the picture is as follows:

there is a constantly shifting emphasis from individualism to social commitment;

emphasis on observing traditional values in schools, families and churches is declining;

evolution means that educational levels are rising – albeit slowly;

there are rising levels of expectation regarding wealth and security;

in general there are declining levels of motivation on achievement and its importance.

So, how does this affect the expectations of people as employees or in the workplace?

In general, the following would appear to be the picture.

Increasingly work would appear to be being designed to minimise the skill required. More and more people are challenging the concept of personal growth.

The pyramid structure of business, with status differentials and chains of command is less popular today. Mutual influence between management and the managed is driving forward a more egalitarian concept in business.

Management's past emphasis on material reward and security of employment is being replaced by management's recognition that social significance of the organisation, the dignity of the individual and the need for both organisations and individuals to recognise their wider responsibilities to a fast-changing world, in all senses of the words.

Old-fashioned career paths are out of date. People now want a very current and new look career structure.

Management's attitude of 'hugging' to themselves the emotional and 'belonging' part of the enterprise has led to the individual's need to share these emotional and rational aspects of the organisation. They offer satisfaction at different levels. These need now to 'belong' to everyone in the organisation.

Management's past policies of encouraging the employee to be as competitive as possible through a reward system and career progression pattern are now being changed to allow for the individual's preference for more communal patterns at work.

Depending on the nature of your work and the organisation to which you belong, your management's attitude may be leading to the increasing alienation of your colleagues and you. In addition, you, yourself, may be feeling increasingly alienated from work itself. What are the results of such attitudes? They are quite simply:

increased social cost of the human output;
decrease in productivity for the organisation.

So, if you or your organisation is in any way in the types of positions described above, one way of earning your keep is to study what you could do to help – both your organisation and yourself.

The Milestones to Remember

There are several milestones to bear in mind when you are considering whether or not you are earning your keep in your chosen job, in business, industry, the professions or whatever. Here are three of the most obvious.

When a person has 'plateaued'

When a person has reached the peak of performance in a particular job or capacity and the supervising managers believe that further improvement on performance may not be possible, that person is thought to have 'plateaued'. This is not necessarily a bad thing; it is a recognition of fact. So, if you are the person who is considered as having reached this point in your career, is it recognised, and what considerations do your employers have in mind?

Managements with whom this issue has been discussed believe that the person who has plateaued can be identified by their inability, at appraisal, to seek new challenges. They, themselves, cannot see challenges within their own job. In these cases enlightened employers make an effort to find a different role if the person involved shows some enthusiasm for a change.

Recognising that the plateau has been reached, organisations do not need to quibble about it – as long as the levels of performance are there. If they are, most managements will try to take a relaxed view and try to get the person to recognise that he or she is happy.

Good management does not need to shake this person out – if the company priorities allow it. They prefer to tailor their expectations for them. With managements using a 'tiering' system, everyone knows what is expected of them and how they are measuring up to this. The top tier – with NatWest it is called the 'E' tier – is for 'high fliers', the emerging top executives, that 1–2 per cent who will go to the top.

The best assessment systems work with maximum transparency with the member of staff concerned, and full, open reporting. NatWest has been using this technique since 1970 and confirm that it works well. They know that they must make proper use of the skills available, which is a responsibility they take very seriously. Robust policies in the culture ensure that – under normal circumstances – people are not let go if they are achieving what is realistically expected. But with approximately 80,000 people to look after in a major clearing bank, things are changing to reflect the economic realities of the day.

Major employers are increasingly proud of the many members of staff who have served the company with twenty-five years or more of continuous service. In the financial sector, and in others, there is increasing awareness of the value of the 'mature' employee with years of experience behind them and the build-up of loyalty to the organisation's culture that can only come from a long span of time spent in that particular organisation, with the networking of friends and colleagues which it brings with it.

It is essential, however, for managements to match their business needs with the right people, young and mature. With some people, who also may be young or mature, it seems as if the world has just passed them by ... They can't be criticised for that. The world – and business – has changed. This is a sober fact of life which needs to be recognised by one and all – no matter at what level you are operating and in which type of organisation.

'Earning Your Keep' – Checklist

To help you to know where you stand in relation to whether or not you are 'earning your keep', here is a simple checklist to complete.

- How long have you been in your present job/function? Did you arrive there as a result of promotion? Or a shift sideways?

- When was your last appraisal? What were the results? How did you do? Can you check it out?

- How do you think you fare by comparison with others in similar capacities at work? The same? Better? Worse? Can you check it out?

- When is your next appraisal? Can you find out, if you don't know? What can you do to improve your position between now and then?

- Do you believe that you have 'plateaued?' If so, can you do anything about it? Can you find out?

- If you believe redundancy may be on the horizon, are you prepared for this? Is it inevitable? Do you know your likely position in terms of time and money? Can you find out? Do you know where to turn for help and advice?

- If you believe retirement is on the horizon, do you know when? Do you know what your position is likely to be financially? Can you find out? Will your financial resources be adequate? Can you check this out?

- Is your family 'on side' and informed about your likely developments as regards redundancy and/or retirement? Do you need to prepare/inform them? Are they supportive?

And finally:

- Is it − in all honesty − within your power to change things? If so, how?

- Then − what would be most fun to do as the next stage in your life? Something where you could develop perhaps quite differently, if you've plateaued or been superseded by someone else who could be better for the job (even if you don't like them).

If you have worked your way through the above checklist you should have faced the facts as to whether you are on a plateau, facing redundancy or retirement. Now is the time to be positive. There are still things you can do to ensure that others know that you are earning your keep. Take the positive view. Other steps in the book will be alerting you to your options in relation to positive action you can take in your own interest. But now, here is another suggestion.

The Positive Benefits of Networking

Networking means consciously extending your current network of friends and colleagues to include a wider range of people who can positively assist you to earn your keep. If you network well, this contributes by:

- enabling you to support others and enabling them to support you;
- helping you by sharing – information and ideas, as well as problems;
- helping you to adapt your thinking, and you'll discover that if you can't help others, you will be able to suggest people who can;
- helping you to get your message across, in an objective and tactful way;
- enabling you to rehearse points you may later wish to put to the relevant people in your organisation;
- helping you to strengthen yourself;
- helping you to widen your horizons.

You should easily find 'networks' at work, or in your local community. And you should find that they will welcome you with open arms. But there is always another option available to you. This is to start up your own network. It is really quite easy and it only needs a small number of you (from two or three, to five) to agree that you want to go ahead. Ralph Nader, the well-known US consumer campaigner, said many years ago that 'Five people is a movement'. There are many examples of organisations setting up on a very small initial base. So, as you see, a very small group of you, working towards common objectives, can set up your own network. And you should find that this can be very productive, interesting and lead to positive benefits for you all.

As one illustration of how a network works and what it can achieve, I know of one distinguished businesswoman who was having difficulty in her job because her senior manager could not see the extent of her contribution. He simply had a narrower scale of vision. She networked to find out if her colleagues were suffering the same difficulties. She discovered they did. As a result of a few discussion sessions with them they produced an action plan for dealing with the problem – and followed it through to a successful conclusion. On the way they had a lot of fun and discovered a lot more about their colleagues, and were able to work better together and to become more productive to the organisation as well. It is natural that advancement followed for her and her colleagues.

So good networking can pay off . . .

In the USA networking is more formally developed than it is in the UK. But, increasingly, its value is being recognised by individuals who are keen to make progress in their chosen careers and by enlightened managements understanding the importance of helping individuals to 'grow' as human beings.

Remember

- Whether or not you are earning your keep depends only in part on your employers – *you* can influence and affect their opinion.

- Positive action on your part can ensure that your employers gain an accurate and postiive opinion of your contribution to the organisation.

- Apathy, inaction and sending the wrong messages can cause others to 'sell you short' at appraisal time.

- Today no one has a God-given right to a job. You have responsibilities – to yourself and to your employers – to ensure that your contribution is recognised and accurately assessed.

- It is important for you correctly to establish your employer's expectation of your performance. A good starting point is a careful study and appraisal of how well you are performing against the job specification for the job/function you are currently carrying out.

- Effort you make in this area will reap rewards – if you go about the task objectively and consistently.

- If you are stuck, think widely about yourself, your needs, and what would be enjoyable as well as earning money by fulfilling an unsatisfied market need.

- As Vincent Duggleby says, 'Don't be one of those people who, on their way to the top, forget their responsiblities to those below them.'

- And, finally, in the words of Professor Thring, 'Take a great deal of trouble with genuinely friendly personal contacts. It is very worthwhile.'

STEP 7

▲

ACHIEVING STATUS

> While, through your working life, you will be able to try to ensure that your worth is recognised, it is only when others preach this gospel for you that it will be seen that you have 'arrived'!
>
> This step looks at what you, yourself, can do to hurry this process on. The step explains what is meant by 'status' and how status can be expressed; it relates status to behaviour, ethics and leadership.

To be seeking status may sound unattractive, unpleasant even, and something you perhaps won't want to identify with as a business or life aspiration. But are you right in holding this concept?

Above all, we must be honest with ourselves. Surely, as human beings, we all automatically search for recognition of some sort. It is a basic human urge. The approval of our identified key peer group is important to us. So is it right to duck the question of status and what it has to offer us in terms of work or business progression, and even personal satisfaction?

I think not.

So what is involved?

Achieving status means that you are perceived as being 'sound', your opinions are worthwhile, and your effort is well directed.

What is perhaps even more important, your efforts produce results. It is acknowledged that you can make a contribution in shaping attitudes and developments. As a consequence, many of your ideas (perhaps relating to a new technology or to the importance of personal ethics, for example) get a hearing. You can be identified as one of those key people who can 'make things happen'.

Are these not desirable and worthwhile objectives?

And, in making your contribution, you will be building up your reputation – not as an end in itself, but as a component to the worthwhile tasks and projects with which you have become identified.

What is wrong with that? Status, after all, is only a part of being known to be a person who makes things happen. And that quality is universally admired in an individual.

So this matter should lie very close to your heart – not because you have achieved status, or sought it. And, however much respect you may have earned, you may not have become a 'front page' personality, chairperson of a multinational or some other dignitary – you may have received more modest recognition! But you should recognise the value of status in empowering you to get things done.

Many of us have always tried to make things happen. But sometimes we go about it the wrong way. Perhaps we are always seen as the 'uncomfortable' person in the team, the one with the novel but 'awkward' ideas – and stubborn with it!

As a result, although many of our ideas are – in the fullness of time – put into operation, perhaps we lost out : others made money or went rapidly up the ladder. Do we mind? Most of the time perhaps not, but sometimes it must have hurt.

Asked perhaps to write a strategy paper for an industry do we discover later that it had been quietly buried as, in the opinion of distinguished members of the group, 'He or she has put the fox in with the chickens again!'

Never mind – some of the concepts put forward then are perhaps now being implemented and, as they say, better late than never!

But being the grain of sand in the oyster, the odd man/woman out, does have its moments too! And they frequently more than balance for the others . . .

Experiences of others, on the matters of success and achieving status, can be highly relevant to you, as a reader of this book. Here are some comments which will be of interest.

From Barbara Barkovitch, a successful US consultant, 'My criteria have become independence, respect (including self-respect), intellectual stimulation, social significance, and flexibility. In the longer-term future I would like to be able to be somewhat more contemplative (e.g. write or teach) and, perhaps (I have mixed feelings about this) re-enter public service.' Barbara also comments that she found it very difficult to make the transition from government to the private sector.

Janet Brady comments 'Remember that status and success breed envy, and often destruction.'

Tom Douglas, a distinguished consulting engineer, spells out the requirement to approach each problem or opportunity with a healthy degree of scepticism. While James Haswell, the original insurance ombudsman, comments that the lasting affection of one's subordinates is far more important than that of the people to whom one is responsible. As he puts it, 'This is because, if one has the first, the subordinates will see to it that one has the second, if given the chance.'

The Key Components

It is perhaps as well to start with a definition of status. According to the *Concise Oxford Dictionary* status is 'social position, rank, relation to others, relative importance'. It is useful, therefore, to know where you stand in the pecking order. Find out by asking yourself these questions.

Do I know my social position?
If I don't can I find out?
Do I want to bother?
Am I comfortable with my rank in relation to others?
Do I want to change it? How?
Do I want to bother?
Is my relative importance a factor of significance to me?
If so, why?

Answering these questions will give you an indication of whether and how much you care about status.

Some categories of status

We have all enjoyed the glib and sometimes very funny books about status and also newspaper, magazine and TV reviews of what is 'in' and what is 'out', 'who' is in and 'who' is out. But there is a serious side to it. If status is important — perhaps to reflect adequately the job or profession in which you are engaged — then it could be irresponsible not to look at the matter in some depth. After all, most professional institutions exist to maintain and improve standards — and thus they regard status as important. Here are some guidelines which should help.

The background factor

Background is a major factor. Examine yours and decide honestly whether it helps or hinders your path to the top. This doesn't mean to say that you are ashamed of a humble beginning, or have an inferiority complex about your early education or the fact that you can't play polo. It simply means that you need to face facts. The present position is made up of one's upbringing, education and the world's effects on one. What is lacking should be made up by one's own efforts. 'Chips on the shoulder' will only benefit your competition.

This book has already indicated in more than one chapter that one of the important keys to success in life is to 'be yourself'. Remember this as you review your position with regard to your current and hoped-for future status.

Intellect and education

Intellectual status doesn't really have anything to do with a top-ranking college or even university education. Having said that, it is useful to know whether or not you have any intellectual ability and this is easy enough to find out through the common rating tests for IQ, ability and performance.

The home and personal scene

Where and how you live, alas, often says more about you than almost anything else. Unquestionably the home environment is important. Here in the UK we are still very focused on this point. We may even take it to extremes. If you live in an old rectory, a converted stable block, or an old mill house, this is considered 'interesting' to say the least. That is not to say that living in a flat is decidely uninteresting, but the type of block and where it is will need to be taken into account before you get the 'green' light on status.

We could go on for ever. Some counties are considered better than others, some parts of town rate more in status than others, and so on. This subject takes in the clothes you wear, the food you eat, and where you go on holiday, as well as the type of car you run, for example. You may feel you are above all that – but, too often, the result is affected by 'inverted snobbery', or feelings of inferiority in others.

You shouldn't dismiss the matter of status out of hand. Human beings are sociable animals and it is very likely that you will find some of your close friends among those you work with in your chosen career, job or profession. It is not surprising that similar types of people live and work in similar circumstances. So you will find you will relate more comfortably with those who share the same likes and dislikes, and 'status' with you. Anyway, others will judge you whether you like it or not.

Remember, too, that improving your profile outside the organisation you work for (but within your chosen field) can improve your status.

Status at work

If you are young, naturally you will be more interested in status-related matters than if you are older. You still have many choices in front of you, and it is possible that you will be influenced by the different status in the workplace. The ladder of status here has been defined again and again. In business generally it used to be felt that working in the City had an extra dimension, a glamour, an additional status – but I wonder if that still holds true? A board

130

director of a public company clearly has status – and he or she will have power, authority, and probably the status and perks that go with that. What are other rungs on the 'status' ladder, and other types of status?

In business:
- being a 'senior manager' conveys status;
- being a department head conveys status;
- being sent on management development courses by your organisation conveys possible future status.

Being a member of the professions conveys status, some more than others.

In the professions:
- being a chartered accountant conveys status;
- being a barrister conveys status;
- being in medicine conveys status – being a consultant is very prestigious and you should have the bank balance that goes with it!

But the balances are changing – try looking ahead.

Writers, artists, scientists and even foreign correspondents have status, but it is suggested that other journalists and politicians are not so fortunate. Down at the bottom of the status ladder come the public relations consultants, estate agents and surveyors, and perhaps private detectives.

Politicians are in a world of their own. Most opinion polls will agree that, as a breed, they have little public favour. Nevertheless, they constantly underline their status. Perhaps they achieve it? For myself I am cynical on this point!

It may be unkind and it may be unfair, but things can be like that. As has been said many times, 'The "facts" are not the actual facts – the "facts" are what the people perceive the facts to be.' So if your chosen job or profession is one of those endowed with less status than some, you should be aware of this and compensate as much as possible to ensure that you protect your own interests for the future – and perhaps raise the status of your own calling.

If you are in a career with a perceived low status, what do you do? Can you do anything, in fact, to raise the status of your career single-handed? While, realistically speaking, as an individual you can do little, if you want to do something you certainly can – in concert with a few initially, but a growing band of like-minded people. The challenge of improving the status of a career, a calling or profession is ideally suited to networking. And such networking can be useful in the wider context too. This type of issue lends itself supremely well to promotion through the editorial columns of the specialist press, your local paper, the national media. But detailed planning is needed to set out the objectives, a realistic strategy and a programme for action.

Remember, though, that embarking on raising the status of your industry, profession or specific calling is a long-term matter. It takes years to make significant progress. Remember, too, that status is seen differently in different countries. For example, engineers are considered as very worthwhile professionals with a high status in Germany, Japan and in the US. In the UK, alas, they are not given the credit – or status – they deserve. The prestigious, highly qualified – and educated – chemical engineer is often thought to be of equal value to the television repair man, who is also called an 'engineer' by ignorant members of the public. In the EC, however, they are addressing the matter of improving and recognising the status factors as far as engineers are concerned. They now identify the well qualified and leading edge engineer with the prefix 'Eur. Ing.'

Status and body language

Like everything else, body language is an important indicator of status. How you walk, how you sit, your manners at table, give away clues about your status. Add to this your demeanour, your confidence level and how you present yourself to others you may be with at the time, and you will see that they are able to fit the pieces into the jigsaw and decide for themselves about your status.

For all these reasons – if not for the more personal reasons related to your own standards – it is important to ensure that you have a good, personable and confident 'presence' at all times. So what are the main and key elements to check?

Here is a simple list.

Personal appearance and dress – ensuring that this is good but not 'over the top'.

Vocabulary – too colourful language should be avoided, but don't be dull!

Handwriting – if you don't know the ins and outs of graphology buy a simple book to put you wise! It's not just nonsense – legibility and style are important, and a courtesy to the reader. Illegible signatures are 'out' and frequently despised.

Manners – at all times these should be good and courteous. It is important never to lose your temper with those who may be subordinate to you in any context. Those who do it for deliberate theatrical effect have to be very skilled to be successful.

Personal material such as visiting cards, letterheads etc. – these should relate to the 'image' you wish to project and be consistent with it. It is here that people can go very wrong, spending too much money and ending up conveying an impression which is the opposite of what they intended!

Any personal 'accessories' – such as briefcase, luggage, even personal jewellery such as watches and rings, should not be flamboyant but quiet, 'elegant' and in keeping with your overall image.

Status and behaviour

Your behaviour gives others substantial clues as to your status. The person who really has status is very often the man or woman who appears to be quiet, modest, assured, listens well, treats all people the same – those below and those above – in the status hierarchy. He or she will generally be recognisable as well read, informed on the narrow and wide issues of the day, having a full and stable family or outside-work life with many non-business interests. In general, too, they will be identified with one or more worthy causes.

You may be sure that the person who has status will *not* be obviously 'hoovering up' the future useful contact at a cocktail party, will *not* pass around visiting cards like confetti on such an occasion, will *not* spend two-thirds or more of the time talking to you at a first meeting to ensure that you understand how important they are and what they do for a living. On the contrary, the person who has status will be seeking to draw you out in conversation, to understand more about you, and the effect should be that you end up impressed by him or her because of this!

So, how do you fare in this context? The checklist below should help you to find out.

Have you achieved status, or are you on the way to achieving status?

Do you like meeting people?
Are you a good listener?
Are you interested in other people's lives?
Would you say you are quiet and dignified, or flamboyant and extrovert?
Have you got outside interests?
Do others seek your opinions?
Do you receive more invitations than you can accept?
Do people come up to you when you enter a room?
Are people often trying to enlist your support for their worthy causes?
Do you like people?

If you have answered the questions raised above you will have learnt something about your attitude to status, and how important it could be in achieving your overall objectives in your working life. It is really worth looking hard at how you can make status work for you – to help you to meet your aims, and in the wider context, too, to help you in your role as a citizen.

Of course it is possible to have status if you are a 'loner', or if you are a 'maverick', even if you are unacceptably extrovert. There are always exceptions to the rule. The above checklist should really be used as a starting point to stimulate your thinking. At the end of a short spell thinking about the matter – say twenty minutes – it should have been possible for you to have decided if you have status, if you want status, and indeed if you need status in order to fulfil yourself in relation to your expectations and stepping-stones to your particular top.

Status is not forever

Finally, there are some important points to remember about achieving status.

As much as you can do to help yourself – even over a long period of time – to achieve status in the minds of your peers, you cannot award status to yourself. It has to be given to you by others.

Status can be a very fleeting quality. For all those who have achieved status, it is only the minority who retain it for a long period of time. If you can, be very sensitive as to whether your position is improving or declining.

And be sensitive, too, to the fact that status is achieved because others can recognise in you that important and unique 'extra dimension' – it could be in your capacity to think, to share, to give, to make things happen. Any effort to build must be on secure foundations; seeking to acquire recognition or status which is built on flimsy foundations is easily seen through and the person who is following this course can end up very much the poorer in all senses of the word as a result.

Status and ethics

In a society that is increasingly confused as a result of global change on many fronts, from economic to political, from environmental to social, the matter of personal ethics becomes more important every day. Ethics and status meet on several levels, so it is well for you to recognise where you stand on the subject of ethics.

What are business or professional ethics? This is the first subject we have to address.

Put simply, ethics is the science of morals, rules of conduct and the basis for conforming to recognised standards. Ethics constitute the principles by which people can live together successfully in a sustainable society. To many ethics can be quickly explained as 'Doing as you would be done by'.

So how do you, as an ethical citizen, translate the all-important subject of ethics into your day-to-day behaviour? And does this affect your status in the workplace?

The answer to the second question is an unequivocal, 'It helps ... sometimes very substantially, to get your value recognised.'

Here is a draft code of ethics for you to consider, and adapt to your particular circumstances as necessary.

Code of ethics for a responsible citizen

The individual should be aware of the importance of the following.

- Tell the truth. How else can you live with yourself, let alone with your friends, neighbours and colleagues?
- Have a philosophy – a set of beliefs and values which drive you. Ensure that these are known by friends, neighbours and colleagues.
- Realise that all colleagues know where you stand – on your beliefs and priorities.
- Err on the side of communicating too much rather than too little.
- Be approachable. Never refuse to talk. Never fail to keep a promise.
- Know the value of time.
- Be sensitive to all matters of pollution and waste.
- Trust and earn trust.
- Show up. Be visible.
- Initiate projects – for the organisation, for the community.
- Help others.
- Recognise the need to return personal value for money – to employer, colleagues at work and in the wider context. See and think widely, around and ahead of the present situation.
- And finally, put all of the above into practice.

So, having studied the above suggestions for a personal code, write out your own version and keep it somewhere prominent as a reminder of the standards which you have set yourself for personal behaviour. You should find it of practical benefit when faced with a dilemma.

Status and leadership

Status and leadership do fit very comfortably together. Every day you can see examples of people who have achieved one with the other. So let us take a look at this important subject of leadership and draw some conclusions which you should find helpful on your way to the top.

Leadership qualities

The aspiring business or professional leader must possess a strong sense of self-awareness. This includes a deep understanding of his or her personal qualities – for instance, attitude to challenge or risk – as well as matters such as strength of commitment to, and pride in, the work in hand.

Being a leader frequently starts you on a lonely road. This should be recognised. By its very nature, leadership means seeing further ahead and over wider horizons. Because of this, most other people involved in the specific issue will not find it easy to follow the arguments, because the extent of their vision will be shorter and narrower. This can mean that the individual with leadership qualities finds him or herself getting frustrated. As a result, they can be considered stubborn or arrogant by their colleagues. The person who is a true leader anticipates these problems and compensates for them by thinking further ahead, meeting the difficulties with a combination of other qualities which range from charisma and charm, to inescapable logic and force of argument.

Finally, if you are an aspiring leader, you should recognise clearly that what will be achieved directly relates to your contribution to the cause, to your level of commitment, clarity of thinking, determination and accurate targeting of the operations involved. It is also important to realise that 'the buck stops' with you . . .

When asked, 'What is the most important quality of a leader?' the answer of many business leaders was unanimous: 'Physical toughness'. This is a surprising and perhaps not often recognised necessary attribute of a leader. With a little consideration, however, it can be clearly recognised as the most important quality. Leaders need to be physically tough to deal with many factors – from the need to work early and late, to the need to deal with stress, crisis management and opportunity. There are taxing physical demands on the leader – and demands, too, on the family of a leader. These thoughts should be borne in mind if you are set on that particular path.

Remember

- The subject of status is important – so don't dismiss it.

- In trying for your own particular 'top' you need to know where you stand on the status ladder, and whether you want to improve your position.

- The signals you will be giving others may be the opposite of those you intend.

- The signals conveying status are many and varied – take the trouble to recognise them – in yourself and check them out in others.

- It may be that being very good at one's job, with the other attributes subconsciously to match, is the real mark of status.

- If you don't need to bother about status you may well have it! The fabulously rich Nubar Gulbenkian, on being asked what sort of status he had, is reputed to have replied 'enviable'. Lord Rothschild, on being told this, is reported to have replied 'Our motto is "service" and by God we get it!'

- Status is related both to ethics and to leadership. Recognise where you stand in relation to both these important matters.

STEP 8

————▲————

INCREASING YOUR VALUE

> It is important to increase your value, and the 'price' you get for your work at every stage of your working life.
>
> This step becomes more important when you have passed through other, earlier steps. It is at this time that the perceptions of others have a direct influence on whether or not you achieve the success you seek.
>
> The step covers the importance of taking a wide view: it discusses gaining recognition; self-development; and gives advice on how to increase your value.

The value of the individual human being is only recently being recognised as the central and key component to profitable and worthwhile business. Over past years systems, technology and the autocratic pyramid structure of business were the composite 'god'. Now, thank goodness, business management is increasingly recognising that human beings are more than wheels in a machine, that they are motivated by many values including their own personal satisfaction, and that they will perform best for those organisations who recognise these simple facts. As a consequence there is beginning to emerge – belatedly – new, softer and more gentle styles of business management.

Oh yes, companies will protest that they give high priority to employee relations, employee care, employee development. But, in many cases, it is only a matter of lip service. There is, however, increasing consensus that developing the human being, in personal and human resources terms, increases their value, and that this benefits both them and the organisation for which they work. This thinking has only relatively recently been given the priority it deserves in the great and the good companies of the world. Better late than never! Alas it follows that in business organisations which do not subscribe to good business practices, the value of the human beings working there sometimes gets short shrift.

So how do you manage your career, to increase your value both to yourself and to the organisation for which you work? What are the stepping stones you can use? How do you develop yourself and achieve a place on the wider stage of your chosen business or profession? And – a tip from Janet Brady – do you recognise the need to develop a stronger, calmer inner self that benefits all around you as well as yourself?

The Key Components

Wisdom is what we all strive to achieve. It is not easy and is difficult to recognise when you have it and, perhaps most significantly, when you do not have it! In the words of Roderick Dewe, 'As long as I was ignorant everything seemed possible. The most difficult task of all was to achieve wisdom.'

Variety is another important factor to consider. Few of us recognise what it can offer. Most of us believe that progressing in a narrow field will lead to the maximum achievement. Perhaps it will. Dr King, however, argues the case for variety, which he finds most fulfilling. He says, 'The accumulation of so many different fields of experience has inevitably generated the holistic approach to life which I now possess.'

The relevance of synergy and taking the wide view

First, it is important to learn the relevance of synergy. An experience gleaned in one area of activity can be put to good use in another, providing the necessary and relevant 'translation' and 'adaptation' have taken place. In a related dimension, time and again – if you look for it – you will find evidence that the addition of one and one can add up to much more than two!

Be aware of this and remember, too, that the more fundamentally important the concept the cheaper it can be in execution, because those who will be prepared to identify with it will do so, not for personal gain, but because they agree on the importance of the concept, and its relevance to logical development in that area. They can enjoy a sense of personal satisfaction in helping to bring it to worthwhile fruition.

At the other end of the scale, remember that a personal reluctance to say 'No' to pleas for help can leave you buried under mountains of work – in the job, and in all the committees and worthy causes with which you have identified.

Retain focus in all your efforts, to ensure that they can contribute to the overall objectives you have set yourself. Above all, ensure you can enjoy what you are doing and can retain enthusiasm for it.

That one life, which we all have, needs to cover many areas. For personal satisfaction we need to know that we are putting things back into society to help make up for what we have received from society. And it is with some sense of satisfaction that we should be able to write that on the record.

Gaining recognition

Increasing your value relates to other people recognising your worth and giving you credit for your achievements. So how do you set about this?

At all levels give more emphasis to your own self-development rather than just technical training, valuable though that may be in itself. At every level individuals should be involved in team tasks which hopefully lead to a better understanding of how the company operates and how they can best perform their job. No one, whatever their level, should be too shy to push themselves forward much more as spokesperson for their role, their profession or their company.

Fitting your aims and those of the organisation together

In earlier steps in this book you should have had the opportunity to get to 'know yourself', to set your goals and objectives, and to consider many factors about the nature of the contribution you can make to the organisation for which you are working. It is now time to see how your aims differ from or complement those of your organisation. How do you set about this?

Today, most companies, and even academic establishments, have prepared and issue widely a 'mission statement'. This is really a broad statement of the nature of the business or activities, their values and their objectives — where they are going and what they are trying to achieve. If you take this statement, and the personal statement which you have prepared on personal priorities, and examine one against the other, you will get an idea of just how well you 'fit' with the organisation for which you are working. You may discover that you and the organisation are quite incompatible. If this is the case, you should take the matter seriously. Consider the three possible options. One: you can stay and change so that your aims can be consistent with those of your organisation. Two: you can try to change the organisation, but this could be difficult if not impossible. Three: you can seek work elsewhere. One thing is for sure, you have a major problem on board, so recognise it as such!

Self-development — how to set about it

Self-development is really a matter of continuing education. It is the sensitivity to the need to widen your horizons, to develop new interests, to engage in other useful 'extramural' activities.

Why is this important? The simple answer is because it 'grows' you as a human being. We can all think of that boring person we know who is narrowly focused, either because all they think of is work, or if there is an outside interest it is so all-embracing that it becomes the only subject they talk about. Human beings who take a wider interest in the world they are living in, who seek to participate and to contribute, bring to all their interests that important extra dimension. It makes them interesting, they are seen to be involved — and they are valued.

So, assuming you want to be involved in a continuing education programme, where do you start?

Genius has been explained as knowing 'what to copy when'. It is a good description. Inventing from scratch is difficult, time-consuming and costly. The recommendations given below on how to approach a continuing education programme have been made after looking at the way some important professional bodies set about the task.

1. Structured courses can be easily researched. Some of these may be of interest to you. To find them talk to the relevant professional or trade body in your sector of activity. Or buy the specialist journal in that area. Your local adult education institute or college may also be able to help. Also you could try your local newspaper, TV station or radio station.

2. Then, consider what other qualifications could be useful on top of, or to buttress, your basic professional job skills. You need to think about this carefully, not only to widen your skills base, but also to help your development as time goes on. For example, as well as a basic degree (if you have one), and corporate membership of the relevant professional body, would an MBA add useful further education? Or would membership of the BIM (British Institute of Management) or the IOD (Institute of Directors), for example, mix you in with the right people to rub shoulders with during your development forward and upward? This thinking applies equally in medicine, say, or art, music, politics or social work, as well as in commerce. Quite often employers will pay, or help pay, for the courses or memberships, when they can appreciate that it enhances your value. In due course this may lead to promotion and salary increases. Additionally, there may be charitable trusts related to your sector of activity who may be prepared to help with funding a specific educational effort by a gifted person who has not the resources or ability to find funding elsewhere.

   But, even if your organisation does not help in practical terms to increase your value, there is a lot that you can do for yourself. Membership of the local junior chamber of commerce has helped many young people to increase their value. There are also many courses available through the local adult education institute which can be of practical use. It really depends on you to determine your own action plan.

3. Joining the relevant community organisation, and establishing yourself on a committee of this, is another useful avenue to explore. The routes outlined above should also lead you to identify these organisations. Try to establish the name of the current chief executive and/or chairman of the organisation you are interested in and approach them on the telephone for the best chance of success.

4. Reading the right books and other publications is, of course, most useful. You will find there is generally one leader (book or magazine) in each specialist sector, so try to identify this.

5. Attend the significant events – conferences and exhibitions – of the area in which you are interested. This leads to a greater understanding of the nature of the key current issues to be faced. The breaks in the conference schedule, for coffee, lunch and tea, offer useful opportunities for 'networking' with those who may be interesting for the future.

6. Finally, set yourself an annual points system to establish the progress you are making. Base this on hours spent. Let us say that you spend two hours reviewing a book or magazine, or attending a conference session, seminar or talk. Give yourself, say, ten points every time you do this. And rate yourself similarly for time spent (perhaps at different rates re points) at courses, committee meetings etc. Assess how much time you may be devoting each month to your continuing education programme – let us say ten hours – and then set a target for the number of points per year which you want to ensure you 'earn' to satisfy yourself that you have taken the matter seriously – let us say 1,000 points. You will be surprised at how satisfying it is to assess the progress of your continuing education in this simple and practical way.

Here is an example – over one month. Let us say that you have set yourself an objective of 'earning' 100 points over the month.

Reading – books, magazines, papers	10 points
Attending two meetings –	
one committee meeting, one other	40 points
Course – attending one session	30 points
Attending conference, seminar etc. once	20 points

So, as you will see, the assessment system is both simple and practical. And you can have the satisfaction of knowing that you are making progress towards your wider objectives.

What Organisations are Looking For

At junior levels success in examinations counts for a lot, as does attention to the job itself. The 'live wire' is always noticed. They tend to be liked and given 'E' for 'effort'. Doing the job well is very important. The annual appraisal picks up on progress made and the individual is looked at hard in relation to how their skills have been polished over the period.

In middle management, performance in the workplace is number one priority. The person's general development and their influence on those around are other key factors that management takes into consideration.

If an organisation has identified someone as having potential, his or her career and preferment follow under the guidance of their career development unit. They have a process to handle this, to see what jobs the individual has done and needs to do, to stretch and develop them. A spell as a personal assistant to a senior executive in the organisation may well be a possibility. This enables the bright young person to learn a further range of skills, to benefit from 'networking' by working for someone high up in the organisation and watching how it is done.

As part of the programme many managements arrange for another executive in the organisation to become a personal contact to the promising young person, their 'grandfather' or 'mentor'. The idea is that he or she is there to help and discuss all matters of concern or interest to the young executive.

Large organisations do, of course, operate formal training courses to increase the value of the young executive. These include coverage of technical, behavioural, personnel functions, matters of excellence, essential management skills and technical competence. They can then see just how these bright young executives are developing and increasing their value to themselves as well as to the company.

A large organisation has to ensure that what they do is done well. Anything less can be a real killer. Right now, every business is having to look much harder at its cost base. Personnel has to be in support of the business. Organisations are not running a career development and progression factory – they are running a business. The fact that they get to promote people or give them career development is because there is a business to be run and they are making sure they have the skills to run that business. Otherwise, they could well finish up with the establishment of a super management development programme, without achieving much in terms of the development of the business itself!

In terms of increasing the value of their staff, large organisations are aiming for people with certain skills and creative ability, and thus development comes naturally. In some cases – as with NatWest, for example – they have also looked at the senior jobs within the organisation and have identified the basis of competences important to them. NatWest plan then to have the top jobs competence-based and assessed so that senior jobs in the bank are matched to the same criteria. After they have done that they plan to do skills audits – to identify the skills needed for the particular job.

Naturally, large organisations are also looking at the cross-fertilisation of skills in mature people and intakes from other disciplines at mature ages.

For management development programmes to be successful – and to increase the value of the individuals – there is a need for the active and visible support of the executive management of the organisation. If they do not listen then it will be jiggered!

If You Want to be Your Own Boss

Many of us find that every now and then we have an idea which we think is particularly appropriate for development into a business of our own. What are the key factors you should consider before you step into this exciting but dangerous territory?

Again, it starts with you. You must know what you have to bring to a new venture; no one else can be involved at this stage. You have to know whether you have the capability to start and run your own business. Having a gut feeling that you can do it and will be good at it is simply not enough. Here is a list of questions which you should answer honestly to clear your mind about your position.

Why do you want to start a business?
Is this a new, or an old urge?
What is new, worthwhile and/or useful about your concept?
Will there be a market for it?
What expertise have you got (or can you get) for the venture?
Is it appreciably better than other people's?
Are you energetic?
Can you work long hours?
Can you cope with the worry and insecurity of running a business?
Have you got the resources financially? Can you get them?
Are you good at money management?
Can you cope with business administration?
Are you a confident person?
Can you take criticism?
Can you plan effectively?
Are you self-disciplined?
What real knowledge, skill and experience would you bring to the new venture?
Do you know what you don't know?
How good is your health?

Answering these questions should give you an idea of whether or not you can stand on the starting grid in relation to looking realistically at starting a business and/or being your own boss. Your options if you want to pursue this path, are set out in Part

3, Appendix 9 where you will find information on the different types of organisation involved, and a note of first steps, including the need for a business plan, setting objectives for the business, deciding its strategy, finances, operations and marketing.

If you do decide to press ahead it is certain that life won't be dull and boring! It could, indeed, become very exciting and rewarding in all senses of the words. It is important, though, to be eminently practical and realistic about the whole matter before pushing any 'Go' button.

Increasing Your Value through Innovation

Today's business environment is undergoing fast-moving changes. The management of that change is central and key to the development of a successful business. It follows that innovation is increasingly recognised as the life-blood of the business that is determined to exist and succeed in tomorrow's demanding environments.

So if you believe that you are capable of innovating, how do you set about it? Above all, what is the right way to 'sell' your new concept so that its value can be recognised and you can be seen to increase your worth in the eyes of your colleagues and superiors?

Here is one analogy which you could find useful.

Innovation is change in human activities, and the process of carrying out change. The sum total of all innovation would constitute **evolution.**

Invention is discovering unexpected ways of doing things, and is only one of many components of **innovation.**

It has to be recognised that radical changes are likely to incur other changes on the way, and that sometimes these other changes are not recognised at the early and important stage.

In this way much of the resource allocated to innovation can be wrongly directed and, in Britain certainly, there have been many illustrations of major, publicly funded, attempts at innovation, having either a fundamental flaw or running out of the necessary funding at the critical stage when 90 per cent of the work had been done and as a consequence all – or nearly all – of the benefit has been lost. Some examples which come to mind include the Gambia egg scheme, the Black Knight and Blue Streak missiles, the TSR2, BR's 'tilting' train and the VC10, to name a few. Perhaps this list should also include the Community Charge!

If you are considering trying to create an innovation it is as well to bear the above points in mind at all times. How can this be done?

Consider the matter of entering a dark room. You cannot see at all. You have no idea of the size of the room, of its shape, of its attractive and unattractive features.

Armed with a torch, you can light up a particular area, perhaps a corner. You find it an attractive area – but could the area on the other side of the room be more attractive? How do you set about lighting up the whole room before you decide what to do with its attractive features and how to handle those which do not appeal to you?

It is much the same with attempts at innovation. Someone has a new concept – it throws light on a particular area. But related and wider thought could determine that there are twenty other concepts to be considered. Some could be much more important and attractive from many points of view. It is up to you, as the innovator, to set about lighting up the whole room before committing resources to the corner which has been illuminated by your new concept.

Priorities to be Considered in Relation to Increasing Your Value

Here are some questions to consider in relation to whether or not you are increasing your value at the moment, intentionally or unintentionally.

Yes No

Have you received praise from colleagues – written or oral – over the last six months?

Have you ever entered into any contest or competition which related to suggestions for innovations or improvements at work?

Have you written to your local or national paper, or technical or trade journal, with suggestions on narrow or wide topics and had these published?

Have you ever been asked for discussion papers on particular topics, or have you volunteered to prepare these?

Has your opinion been asked on particular issues at work?

Have you been recruited on any minor or major 'think-tank' operations?

Do you find it difficult to put your thoughts down on paper, or to speak at small or large functions?

Has an idea, or a concept which you have developed, ever been adopted by others?

Do you have a folder or file where you log suggestions you may wish to make on topics at a later date – given the opportunity?

Having considered these questions you should be able to judge whether or not you are on the way to increasing your value at work. If you decide that you are not on this path yet, you can consider whether or not you wish to tread it in the future.

Advice on Increasing Your Value

TEN DO'S

1. Always say 'Yes' to a new opportunity within the organisation.
2. Join networks which promote your interests.
3. Enjoy your work. If it isn't fun, do something about it.
4. Accept that there are no long, linear career paths.
5. Go on learning.
6. Remember intuition is as valid a method of decision-making as rational analysis.
7. Try to understand the values of the corporation and, if you don't, say that to your manager.
8. Be constantly aware of new and better ways in which you could do your job. Do everything possible to simplify organisational structure and remove barriers which may prevent easy communication.
9. Go for an open door policy, an open plan office.
10. Develop the freedom within your role to do it the way you wish to do it.

SIX DON'TS

1. Don't expect 'normality'. A healthy organisation changes constantly.
2. Don't work for a company whose values/products you don't respect.
3. Don't assume that there is nothing you can do to make your job more satisfying.
4. Don't automatically assume that if you haven't received promotion it's because you are a woman, a member of a minority group etc.
5. Don't accept a situation where there is concrete evidence of prejudice. Complain to the right authority and show evidence.
6. Don't bully and don't accept bullying.

Finally, some tips from the top. Tom Douglas stresses the need 'to make the most of any and every opportunity you may be offered'. Dr Elizabeth Nelson endorses this and adds, 'Never say

"NO" to any extra responsibility, but at the same time, be absolutely certain of your focus.'

John Patterson, former Chief Executive of National Savings, with a long and distinguished career in the civil service, has some cogent advice for the reader. He says, 'Allow others to build on their strong points as you hoped that your own managers would allow you to do. I believe there is great importance and benefit in sharing problems with people at all levels.'

Martin Smith, a successful industrialist, introduces a new dimension, 'It is of great benefit to have close friends or relationships outside one's immediate professional environment, preferably more experienced than oneself, but who are sympathetic to one's own ambitions. In such a relationship, one is able to get a detached and objective view of how one is shaping up to opportunities that may lie ahead, not necessarily those immediately to hand. Being a loyal part of the organisation is very important. Organisations cannot work without loyalty, but individuals cannot grow without an objective view of where they ought to be going.'

Lady Wilcox echoes the above and adds, 'Put some time every week into work in the public or voluntary sector.'

And, a final word from Lady Phillips, 'Always keep an open mind. And continue to learn – never assume you have all the answers.'

Remember

- Nothing stands still. If you are not increasing your value currently, it is likely that your value is being eroded.

- Businesses and professions do not develop in a vacuum. They prosper because of effort and innovation by people.

- If you have the capacity to innovate you should recognise that you have the responsibility to put this talent to good use.

- Increasing your value to those you work with increases your value to yourself – and should give you a lot of personal satisfaction.

STEP 9

---▲---

MAKING YOUR VOICE HEARD

The steps outlined earlier in this book should have helped you to understand some of the key components which should assist you in getting to the top of your mountain.

As you advance, 'making your voice heard' assumes more importance. It is only now, perhaps, in terms of your progression, that you will be able to give this important matter the time and attention it deserves.

This step addresses achieving influence; the importance of communication and recognition; your image, its significance, and how to manage it are discussed; also the value of becoming an 'expert'.

Making your voice heard should be simple and straightforward. But it isn't. We are often heard saying that the same old faces appear on the 'box', or in the national or trade newspapers, voicing their opinions again and again on this, that and the other issue. It may also seem as if the organisation you work in is always listening to the same people. Most of us sometimes feel we don't get a look in. Why is this? How does it come about?

Making your voice heard seems at times to consist of a series of impossible tasks. But it can be done. How? If your organisation needs to hear your voice, then it follows that you should have something significant to say!

There are, of course, many difficulties on the way. As Dr Alexander King puts it, they come in the way of traditional thinking, unwillingness to change, vested interests and the generally dampening force of the bureaucracy.

Naturally, for others to want to know what you think, you must have an opinion. Or be known as a person who is not afraid of voicing your opinion, when asked. Equally it follows that you should be identified as a person whose opinion is important and relevant, that you have influence, that you are an 'expert' in the area being reviewed.

And it is also logical that you need to be viewed as a 'leader', and that you are a person 'of value'.

So – what is your value? What is important about your opinions? You need to know.

Being in this category can offer opportunities, and it can cause problems, to you and the organisation you work for.

Is your organisation's voice *your* voice? Are your views consistent with the views of your top management or your leaders? It is most important to recognise the relevance of these questions and to know the answers to them. Clearly, the more you share the opinions of your senior management, the easier it makes things, both for them and for you. Beware, though, of becoming a 'Yes' man or woman, for skilled managers can easily see through such hypocrisy. Even leaders of nations have been known to fall because their loyal members of staff told them what they wanted to hear and not what they should have been told in their best interests – and those of the nation.

But making your voice heard is important in another and significant context, too. It is important to you – as a human being. It is important, also, in relation to the positive benefits your opinions could stimulate and translate into action, if expressed in the right way and at the right time.

We remember well the times an opinion is asked for, perhaps by a colleague at work, perhaps by outside organisations, maybe by the media. And the good reasons why the response given is in fact no response at all, just waffle, or even worse 'no comment'. Equally we can all identify those who believe that the organisation they work for sells 'gold bricks' – accepting blindly all the 'official' lines. As a result they could well suffer from the reputation of being boring, people whose opinions don't matter because they can always be predicted, people without minds of their own. Today, happily, things are changing and the fact that human beings – and organisations – do express opinions, accept that they can be fallible and make mistakes, is better recognised and they are not unnecessarily penalised for that.

Today, too, the principle of people speaking on behalf of their organisation and not being just faceless spokespersons is accepted. This is good. What must be avoided, at all costs, is the temptation to fall into the trap of being considered by your colleagues inside the organisation, and those outside whose goodwill you value, as the person who can be relied on to express the 'party line', no more and no less! Being successful at this can be like treading on eggshells; it is not easy, but it can be done.

Knowing when and when not to let your hair down is an important attribute in whatever business or profession you have chosen.

So, how do you get your message across? How can you ensure that you are making an impact?

The Key Components

Influence and power are nothing more than the potential to get things done. Making your voice heard is central to acquiring influence. Influence itself is a part of everything we do, every day. If we use what influence we have ethically, it is a formidable skill. It is critically important to success – in an organisation, in a life. Without the ethical use of influence, quite simply, less would be achieved in the long run. Influence is needed to build the effectiveness of teams, to reach consensus decisions, and to effect and to manage change.

Achieving influence

So, before you consider making your voice heard, you should also think about the broad sweep of influence as an area, and how to achieve it. It is important in this context to consider that, like any powerful force, influence can lead to very substantial achievements. But it is equally important to remember that – because of the power that can be released from the effective use and communication of influence – the morality of its use should be examined on each occasion. It is that underlying morality that can make all the difference. Make sure you use what influence you have for good, in order to benefit people and not the reverse.

So, consider this checklist in order to discover whether or not you have influence, or whether you can achieve it.

	Yes	No
Do you have sound bases for your opinion?		
Is your opinion really relevant to your organisation?		
Do others ask you for your opinion?		
Are you the person first invited to take part when a new working party is being formed?		
Do you offer your opinions often in group discussions? Are the points you make accepted?		
Does the chairperson of the group ask you to introduce the discussion, or to wind it up?		
Do your colleagues 'warm' to you? Do you have friends who are colleagues? Do they ask after your family, your holiday, your health? Often? Not just the 'polite' question in the 'I couldn't care less really' voice?		
Have you been promoted recently?		
Have you offered to develop a new concept, an idea, a programme – and had it turned down? Do you know why it was rejected? Did you find out?		

156

Yes No

Are you asked to see or interview people interested
in entering your sphere of work?

Hopefully, by working through the above checklist you will have
established whether or not you have influence. If you have
influence you must ensure that you exert it for beneficial and
objective reasons which are fully thought through. If you have
discovered you don't have influence, but you want to acquire it,
make a decision that you will work at the matter, and give yourself
a time-scale to achieve progress. Other steps in this book should
help to point you in the right direction for a practical start.

Exerting influence – and getting your message across

In order to exert influence, and to get your message or your
opinion across, you must be an able communicator. You must be
able to make an impact. It follows that if you do not have the
ability to communicate, all can easily be lost. Further, the chances
for progression – in your chosen business, profession or other
career – are poor.

So how do you start to find out whether or not you are a good
communicator? And how do you set about polishing up the skills
you already have?

The stepping stones

There is a simple and obvious relationship between influence,
recognition and communication. The first rung on the ladder is
communication, then comes recognition and that leads up to the
top rung – influence. These are the important stepping stones to
success.

Of course, the nature of your work will have an impact on the
kind of the action you will wish to take in relation to the stepping
stones. However, the principles are probably the same in large
measure, no matter what business or professional activity you may
be involved in.

Communication

Today most of us have very busy lives, with stress taking an increasing toll on us as the world progresses, developing faster and faster in technological terms. While a century ago much time could be spent in teasing out the key messages lying at the heart of an important new concept, today's world demands that we have rapidly to construct those messages so that they are sharp and clear and, hopefully, short and precise.

There are many simple and short (and long and pompous) ways of expressing what needs to be done. Indeed, whole books have been written on this subject alone. Here is a simple formula which could serve you well over the years:

Step 1 Decide what action you wish to stimulate.

Step 2 Decide who needs to hear your message.

Step 3 Decide how the message will be transmitted, and when.

Step 4 Decide what the overall message is.

Step 5 Send it.

Step 6 Ensure it is received.

Step 7 Check the message has been 'heard' accurately and correct it if necessary – there is more distortion possible in the translation of messages, even in a conversation between two people, than you can possibly imagine. The message given is rarely the message received, so be particularly careful to check on this.

Step 8 In due course, check on the result you have achieved.

So remember that making your voice heard is more really than how you say it, and it is not only about the appropriateness or crudeness of your delivery – whether in speaking or in writing your message. It is about the clarity of your thinking initially, and the effect your message actually results in, the action it stimulates, from others and from yourself. The elegance of the delivery of the message follows from that.

The tools of the trade in relation to making your voice heard are very much the same as for marketing and selling. You will need to know how to make more of media opportunities, whether or not you need media training. You will need to assess how good you are at putting your thoughts down on paper, whether you are good on your feet and so on. Step 5, *Selling Yourself*, also deals with effective communication and should help you with more detail. You should also look at the Action Plan for 'You Limited' in Part 3 (Appendix 8) and information on preparing your CV (Appendix 5).

Recognition

Achieving recognition relates specifically to the quality of your thinking and the decisions you take with regard to your personal strategy, and the tactics you use to get your messages across. Very frequently people get all hyped up with the importance of the message they want to transmit. As a result they sort out the message, but then fail to get the desired result because they have expended a great deal of effort on the fourth part of the exercise and neglected the first. They have failed to recognise the importance of the tactics they use to get their message across. How the message is 'packaged' and delivered, and the timing, is critical in getting the desired result.

So, how do you tread warily on the stepping stones in these dangerous waters?

Here are some guidelines which may be helpful.

1. Do remember that you want to be taken seriously − those already at the top are always on the look-out for the man or woman who has the talent to join their select little group, now or in the future. The worthwhile ones want to hand on their own jobs so that they can go upwards themselves.

2. Bear this in mind at all relevant times. Also bear in mind the fact that managers are well skilled to recognise the right signs ... Only too often people believe that their managers are uninterested in identifying those with talent. The reverse is actually the case.

3. Ego is important, so recognise this. Anyone who is a leader or who wants to be a leader has a well-developed ego. This is

known and expected. You yourself need some. But ego can lead the unwary into many traps as it expresses itself – revealing many 'giveaway' signs. Watch yourself in this regard. Warning signs include the simple use of too many 'I's in your explanations of developments, either verbally or on paper. Above all, check up on your letters, ensuring that too many paragraphs do not start with the tell-tale I! (Egoists are personal 'pushers': egotists use 'I' all the time. The latter makes the former less effective.)

Remember to rein in the ego so that it is a positive tool you can use for benefit, and ensure that it doesn't let you down on that important occasion.

4. Know how to identify and embody the values that your organisation wants and needs. Make your contribution worth while.

5. Study your own communications profile, check on which elements of it are good, and how you can improve them. Above all, check on which elements are bad, where you are weak, and decide to work on eliminating any weaknesses. Here is a checklist to help you look at specific areas.

	Yes	No
Can you make a good speech? How good?		
Can you speak impromptu if asked? How well?		
Can you think on your feet?		
Can you recover swiftly if something has gone wrong with the presentation?		
Can you write well and fluently?		
Do you contribute to relevant publications?		
Can you express an argument well on paper? Logically?		

	Yes	No
Can you identify opportunities and threats?		
Can you analyse them?		
Can you produce solutions to problems? More than one?		
Can you construct flexible solutions?		
Do you contribute well in a committee or working party context?		
Do you seek additional responsibility?		
Do you pay attention to your appearance? Your speaking voice?		
Can you persuade others to your point of view?		
Can you recognise your mistakes and take the necessary action to correct them?		
Can you take criticism and turn it to advantage?		

6. 'Packaging' your message is also very important – you must decide which is the best method and occasion for its delivery. It could be at an organisation function, it could be in a discussion paper or memorandum, it could be at committee. Equally it could be delivered on an informal occasion or even quite privately – it all depends on the receiver and the message. Remember that – particularly in the case of an important, new, creative concept – it is as well to have a record of the message, and where and how it was delivered. You can never tell when that could be important.

7. Remember, too, that you are sending out messages all the time. And that they are different messages. Make sure that some of your messages don't cancel others out! This happens

time and again with companies. As an example, one director makes a presentation to a city audience, explaining that the company is expecting record profits. At the same time, another director is explaining to employees, trade unions, and specialist and local media that the company has to lay off employees and is working short-time. Both messages are at odds with the other and the result is bad for the company. Ensure that the messages you send out are consistent, one with the other.

8. Timing is another critical factor to consider. In relation to achieving results in planting messages about new creative concepts, it is most important. Ensuring that the timing is right is also difficult to determine. Remember that, at the seashore, there is a time when the surf breaks. If you are trying to ride the surf you must judge that moment precisely, to get the exhilaration of the sweeping, fast ride in to the shore. Timing the presentation of an important message has many of the same elements. Ensure that you give it high priority in relation to achieving the result you seek.

Going through the above checklist, and recognising whether you are strong or weak as a communicator, should assist you to know where you stand in terms of achieving recognition. If you decide you are weak at communication you should take a decision to work at it. Refer to Part 3, Appendix 10 to see how to define your own position.

Your image and how to manage it

Recent research (by Harvey Coleman, ex-IBM), across a number of large organisations, identified three factors that determine preferment or promotion:

performance – the quality of your work;
image – the impression you create, of yourself and your work;
exposure – what others know of you.

162

The report indicated that performance, or the quality of the work, contributed only 10 per cent to the decision to promote someone. The image factor accounted for 30 per cent and the exposure factor for 60 per cent. These figures give rise to sobering thoughts.

Image is:

What you **look like**
  Do you look the part?
  Is your manner of dress appropriate?
  Do you appear relaxed and in control?
  Are you confident?
What you **sound like**
  Is your voice quiet and confident?
  Is it clear?
What you **say**
  Is it explicit?
  Consistent?
  Short?

Above all, do all three factors add up to an impression that you are relevant and mature in your thinking, objective and in control?

If you consider the image as a 'snapshot' you won't go far wrong. It is the 'snapshot' of you that someone takes when you come into a room. This takes in what you look like, what you say, how you talk. It leads them to make a general impression about you, filling in from that snapshot a lot of other qualities. These can range from the quality of your thinking, your ability and your worth, in many senses of those words. It can be grossly unfair, quite wrong, overstate what you have to offer, or deny you credit for what you are and what you offer.

It is important that it is as accurate a view of you as you can possibly get. This is very much in your interests. It will help you to achieve your personal objectives.

Give the matter of image the priority it deserves.

Managing your image and improving it relates to setting out where you are now, your current position. It calls for a bruisingly honest appraisal of what you are good at and what you are bad at, and an action plan to improve your position. Here is a table for you to fill in.

Your Current Position

Your image

Appearance	Good and appropriate ☐	Needs attention ☐	Bad ☐
Voice	Good and appropriate ☐	Needs attention ☐	Weak ☐
Verbal communication	Good and appropriate ☐	Needs attention ☐	Weak ☐
Written communication	Good and appropriate ☐	Needs attention ☐	Weak ☐

Tick or delete as appropriate and you will identify the areas where you need to pay attention to improving your position.

Opportunities to build your image

Here you should write down what opportunities you can think of with dates for action by you. Some area to consider are:

> organisational meetings, committees, working parties;
> club meetings;
> conference platforms;
> radio and TV phone ins;
> letters to appropriate media;
> initiation of new group of influence;
> endorsement of work of others;
> contribution of news or feature material to appropriate journals or media;
> initiation of contact with opinion formers in organisation, trade, industry or professional body;
> initiation of appropriate meetings with local councillors, members of parliament etc.

Now you should have an indication of where you stand and the first elements of an action plan to consider.

Making the most of what you have achieved

This area is generally given scant attention. Most of us have developed our CVs and use these as appropriate when the time comes to look at a promotion, job change or new opportunity. We rarely think of polishing our CV up as a document to use in a wider context, but there are ways of doing just that. You should find it a useful tool in your path to your particular top. Certainly, many of the distinguished people who have helped with this book have noted that the opportunity to contribute their thoughts to the book reminded them of their need to analyse just what they had to offer, and how often they had neglected putting this down on paper!

See Appendix 5 in Part 3 for more information on CVs – how to write and present them.

Your achievements

Make a note of what achievements you have already:

- where you have contributed key suggestions which have been implemented;

- improvements you asked for which were granted by your winning the day at the appropriate meeting;

- 'firsts' of record where your suggestions were accepted, resulting in new thinking, or the development of new programmes by those with whom you are working.

Now make a note of where your achievements have been recorded. Were they noted in minutes of meetings? In discussion papers? In the publication of the organisation? In the local or trade paper? In a book or professional journal? On radio or television? If not, it is as if they never existed at all. That is a sobering thought for you to reflect on!

At the end of the day, ensure that all is consistent with the overall objectives which you have earlier decided to try to achieve.

Extending your influence

If you want to extend the influence you have at this time, you need to develop two awarenesses. The first is the awareness to keep up a momentum in your communications, and to ensure that the quality is consistent and high. The second is to ensure that you are not disseminating too many differnt messages in too many different directions. Sharpen the focus. Consider the niche, the key area of interest. Examine the opportunities and resist the temptation to be all things to all men and women. That would be the surest way to counteract any progress you may be making.

Above all, don't try to be too clever. Remember the time it takes to get people to absorb messages, decide their attitude to them and decide to take the action which may be called for. Keep it simple, and short if possible.

Try to construct for yourself an agenda to extend your influence. Identify the areas in which you want to have influence. These could range from the sharp area of your particular work, to your interests in education, art, philosophy, environment, community etc.

As you make progress to extend your influence, your goals may be changing – and you do not need to view this as a bad thing. One of the central priorities to recognise in relation to extending influence is the need to define, redefine and change towards gradually strengthening your own position. The very results you will be achieving as you travel this path will change the context.

Making an impact

Here is a list of do's which should be helpful.

DO plan your progress broadly (not in great detail).

DO decide what action you want others to take.

DO have substance to your message.

DO give enough care and consideration to those to whom you address your message. What are they concerned about? What do they think of you? What would change their thinking to your point of view? What do they expect of you?

DO remember the importance of image. An image is projected, not created. You have an image, whether you like it or not. This image of you builds in the minds of others, irrespective of what you want. Make sure it works for you and not against you. As Lord Thorneycroft said back in 1978, 'Image is what you are'. Remember that. If you try to be what you are not, the chances are that you will fail.

DO decide if you need help. If you do, take an immediate decision to get it. You will only benefit as a result.

DO remember, above all things, that a message – to be successful – must be short, sharp and repeated many times. It must fit into the receiver's psyche.

Becoming an expert

Most people like to put other people in 'boxes' and carry a brief 'shorthand' view of them, as we said earlier, a 'snapshot'. Often they confuse the real person with the snapshot. For example: 'He is a thinker'; 'She is a doer'; 'He is a status seeker'; 'She is frightened of her own shadow'. Related to this is the area in which they 'box' that person: 'He is a boffin'; 'He is an expert on . . .'; 'She is on her way to the top'.

So, to make an impact and get your message across, you should consider the snapshot you would like others to have of you. Being known as an 'expert' in a particular area, the person to talk to on that subject, the person who is in touch, who knows what to do or whom to ask, can be important in this context.

Becoming an 'expert' does not necessarily mean hours of study, years of sitting examinations. But there is a common factor – a curiosity to know more about the particular area. It also means being in touch with those who really know. Think of it as being a spider in the middle of the web, being at the heart of the debate in that area. That automatically gives you value in the eyes of others.

How to do it couldn't be simpler:

– choose your area;
– read up about it;

- join the relevant organisation/s;
- make sure that others who need to know realise that you are prepared to help them if they approach you for advice or specific help;
- have opinions about specific aspects of your area of expertise;
- express your opinions – and get your messages across, as relevant and appropriate in your wider scheme of things;
- commit your time – as much as may be needed.

Further advice comes from Tom Douglas. He says, 'Equip yourself as best you can for the task you wish to undertake.' Vincent Duggleby adds, 'Remember to have the humility needed to question assumptions in every walk of life and to communicate this to others.' Professor Thring underlines the need for consultation. He advises, 'Consult widely before taking an important decision.'

Remember

Harvey Thomas, who changed the face of political presentations in the UK in the 1980s, has said it all in his version of the ten commandments.

1. See yourself as you really are.

2. Know your objective.

3. Have an overall picture in mind before you start on the details.

4. Work out your routine plan.

5. Rehearse.

6. Take your audience by the hand and lead them along with you.

7. Win hearts – then minds.

8. Keep it simple.

9. Be enthusiastic.

10. Be yourself.

STEP 10

———▲———

THE ASSESSMENT

In this last step you should be able to reach an assessment of the progress you have made, or can make, towards your objectives.

In this step we also look at strategies for the future, and give a distillation of views from the top, and from those on the way to the top.

Finally, in this step the important question is examined – is it worth it?

Through the pages of this book you should have obtained the information to help you to know yourself, to know where you stand, what you need to do in order to secure the type of life which is right for you, and to enable you to get the happiness and satisfaction from it that is the ultimate aim of us all. If you are better able to identify the type of mountain you wish to climb, and how to climb it, also to view the wider horizons which could lie beyond it – then this book will have succeeded in its task.

It could be, however, that you still consider there is much to be done in order to achieve your objectives, even if these are now a little clearer to you.

So what do you need to do?

Your assessment

The following checklist should enable you to identify what action you now need to take.

Yes No

I believe that I know myself sufficiently to be able to cope with the way ahead. ☐☐

I believe that I know where I stand, and where I am going. ☐☐

My goals are clear – I have set them and know how to set about achieving them. ☐☐

My attitude to progressing in my job, to changing direction, to obtaining the necessary qualifications and to continuing my professional education is known to me, and I am happy with it. ☐☐

Can I sell myself as well as I need to? ☐☐

If not, do I know what to do to improve this aspect of my working life? ☐☐

Am I confident that I am 'earning my keep' at work? ☐☐

Am I comfortable with my current status? ☐☐

Do I know how to improve this? ☐☐

Am I sufficiently involved with extramural activities? ☐☐

Or am I involved too much? ☐☐

Am I confident that my value is increasing?

Am I making my voice heard? ☐☐

	Yes	No
Effectively?		

and, finally,

	Yes	No
Do I know what others think of me?		
Am I happy about their opinions of me?		

Filling in this checklist should give you a clear indication of where you need to take action. Earlier pages of the book should have given guidance on the setting of the objectives and the strategies necessary to meet them.

Let us now take a look at what advice is forthcoming from others who have made it to the top or who are on their way to the top.

Views From the Top

In the comments made by the many people and organisations who have helped with the compilation of this book, certain common strands come through which are important to recognise, and which give much food for thought.

The first of these strands is the almost universal view that it is important first to consider yourself as a human being, and to know what is important to you and why. Achievements are looked at mostly in terms of the personal satisfaction which flows from them, rather than the obvious commercial and financial success which may follow.

The second strand is the strong feeling that it was the approval of the parents which was being sought by the successful person. The importance of parental influence in this day and age, when we read, all too often, about the break-up of the family unit, comes as a surprise, but it is none the less welcome for that.

The third strand is the high priority put in making personal relationships work, and in networking with like-minded people which, again, was underlined more strongly than many would have imagined.

Finally, any difficulties they examined were always looked at most objectively, with candid comments that they were probably the fault of both sides involved!

So what advice have those who are at the top for the readers of this book?

Barbara Barkovitch, successful US consultant, draws attention to the need for intellectual fulfilment. She says: 'I decided that it was important to have as much independence as possible, to do something for a living that I found intellectually interesting and socially important. But it is hard to think of keeping up this pace for more than another ten years. I am forty now, and would like to have time to write another book, teach or go back into public service at some point. Since this is already my third career, the thought of a fourth does not frighten me.'

She goes on to comment on the importance of the right personal relationships, 'It is really important to work in a field where you can respect the people you work with and their motivations.'

Janet Brady, a managing director, identifies some of the problems that will be encountered. She warns, 'Avoid believing other people's commitment to be as strong as yours. Also be careful not to allow others to override your "gut" instinct, especially where the hiring of people is concerned.'

Jilly Cooper, best-selling author, underlines the natural and very human need for praise. She comments, 'I always get terribly thrilled when I have letters from other writers to say they have enjoyed something I've written; particularly other journalists, because praise from the professional is always the one you want most.'

Roderick Dewe, well-known public relations consultant, takes a different direction. In relation to being your own boss he stresses the need for the long-term view, 'An entrepreneur must, if he sees any other values than maximising his capital worth through a timely sale, be concerned with passing on what he has created to a second generation'.

Additionally he identifies from his own experience an important area in which to avoid mistakes: 'believing accountancy was an exact discipline and that what your accountant delivered was fact.'

172

Vincent Duggleby, a leading financial journalist, returns to the personal and human priorities. He says, 'Be happy in the work you do, at whatever level. There will be times of frustration, anger and despair, but as long as you can truly say that you have given 100 per cent, then you will be able to put down the inevitable failures to experience. Learn from that experience and do not look backwards to what might have been.

'Trust your judgement and if you do not feel sufficiently confident to do this, then call on someone else whose judgement you can trust. Finally, be honest with yourself (if not with others) over your own shortcomings.'

Peter Hayes, successful businessman, advises from the point of view of running your own business, 'Very few people are cut out to run a business. It needs a lot more than just money, which some people think is all it takes. Don't do it unless you are prepared to become a workaholic. Only do it if you have a bee in your bonnet about something as this "buzz" is what will keep you going.

'If you approach a bank or anybody else to lend you some money to get started in a business, make sure you ask for enough and, having rounded up all the figures, then add 20 per cent just in case, and extend by at least six months the period during which you will make a loss before you actually break even. Then tell the bank manager you have done this – which should impress him greatly!

'Don't leave a secure job to start a business unless your family are supportive – neutral is not enough.

'Whatever it is you want to do, make sure you are superb at it before you even begin, and make sure you succeed first time – nobody will back a loser.'

John Patterson, formerly Chief Executive, National Savings, comments from experience in another dimension, running a large organisation. He says, 'I have never consciously planned to "get to the top", and it has never been one of my life's ambitions. But it has always been essential to my self-esteem to feel that I was making full use of my gifts and experience. And being in charge of a big national institution, when staff had to be led through some very difficult changes and have come through

173

feeling that they are now moving in a good direction has been an immensely satisfying challenge. The full satisfaction can only be felt by the person who is "at the top".

'For me the key point about the "top" is being in charge and having a great deal of freedom to make decisions for my organisation. The word "top" is not one of my favourite management words, but the concept is a vital one. Leading, guiding, communicating and team-building are all key elements of management. But, at the end of the day, one person has to say – "We are going to do this – now let us get on with it".

'The art of leadership is to give all members of the team the same sense of direction. Only the leader can provide it, though other team members may give vital guidance to the leader.'

Michael Rice, specialist on Middle Eastern Affairs, points to the need to act when you are still young. He comments, 'My advice is to do whatever it is you want to do. Start to do it, whatever it is, as young as possible, for much is forgiven those who attempt when young.'

Martin Smith, industrialist, looks at matters from the view of established business, 'Mature professionals know that, in our attitudes, our understanding of society and our technical expertise, we are representative of a moment of time. At the same time, we have an opportunity to contribute to the development of all of those aspects through time.'

Professor Meredith Thring, distinguished academic, advises, again from the personal dimension. He comments, 'My advice is to act outwardly as if it really mattered that you succeed, but inwardly not to take yourself or your difficulties too seriously. Don't regard outer success as the most important thing in life. The quality of your life will matter much more when you lie on your deathbed. This quality is much more measured by creative self-fulfilment, i.e. using your talents to the full, in somehow helping to make a better world, and by loving relationships.'

Jan Walsh, consumer affairs specialist, spells out her perceptions: 'I don't have a concept of achievement or success equalling power. I define "success" as "a combination of personal ethics, professional values and the opportunity to make a difference in one's chosen arena – whether political, commercial or social". Within these parameters there are always new goals to achieve – because the goalposts keep moving.'

One of the mistakes she says she made was 'Believing that leadership was a largely autonomous, Yang-like quality, of course the buck has to stop somewhere, and the titular or team leader accepts that, along with the responsibility for their own achievements and that of their team. But leadership qualities are present in each team member – that's why they are selected – and the sum total of those qualities are as important to the overall effectiveness of a team leader as is his or her own determination, drive and ability to make decisions.'

Her advice for you, the reader, 'As you climb the mountain of success, don't forget to take time to appreciate the beauty of the landscape below and around you, because that's where you came from. There lie the foundations of the mountain and your support as you scale the peaks ahead.'

David Wickes, film and TV producer, draws attention to problems: 'Remember that piling today's problems on top of tomorrow's will eventually sink your enterprise. I wish somebody had told me that when I was young. If they had, I would have been more decisive far earlier.'

He adds, 'Fortunately for me, I was brought up in an atmosphere where the word "maverick" was not a pejorative but an accolade.'

His advice, 'Work hard, sleep well, always believe in yourself and never do anybody down.'

Lady Wilcox, former industrialist and now Chairperson of the National Consumer Council, identifies one of the prices of success. She says, 'There is a price for success, and we must be prepared to accept the responsibility that comes with its privileges. We should remember that only in discipline is there freedom.'

Views From Those Who are on Their Way to The Top

Here are some thoughts from those who are on their way to the top.

Karen Pheasant is young, just entering her thirties. She is highly intelligent and industrious, working as a key executive at the National Westminster Bank. She says that it was her parents who first instilled ambition into her. Her interest in microbiology survived to university, but she then decided that isolated research work wasn't for her and headed off in search of a management traineeship. This took her to NatWest as a graduate trainee and her progress has been swift and sure since then, including the opportunity to attend a full-time MBA course at Warwick University, sponsored by the bank. She puts great store by the development of business contacts through membership of the junior chamber of commerce and other local organisations, also in the need to balance work and private life to avoid stress and broaden horizons.

Here is her advice for the reader.

'DO ...
• Make yourself visible, ask questions, seek high-profile roles, suggest improvements.
• Appear confident.
• Tell people you're aiming high.
• Appreciate the contributions other people can make: their willingness to help will increase in proportion to the amount you listen.
• Learn how to address an audience and chair meetings.
• Keep up with wider developments and their impact on your business.
• Take charge of your own self-development.

DON'T ...
• Bullshit: you may get away with it, but if you're found out, your credibility will be undermined.
• Worry if you make a mistake: admit it, sort it out and don't do it again.
• Be afraid to say "no": providing you can justify it.
• Shirk responsibility: it's your opportunity to prove how good you are.'

Martina Platz is another high-flying young woman. She also took the scientific route at university, graduating with a first-class honours degree in biochemistry from Liverpool University. Fortunate to work first for a boss who was keen to develop young people, she has worked with some of the largest organisations in the country in her current job with Coopers & Lybrand Management Consultancy Services. She says, candidly, that consulting can be quite stressful, particularly if one becomes overloaded with work, and finds one of the key factors to success is to make sure that she manages her time very tightly so as not to overcommit herself. She finds it enormously satisfying to do a good job for a major client which, with demonstrating her professional ability and integrity, is a prime motivator. As with Karen, Martina has found a sponsored MBA most useful to broaden her outlook to be a business-oriented strategic manager. She also believes that it is important to have role models and somebody you can talk to quite openly about work and how things are going. As with Karen, she believes it important to balance business and personal life – in her case time spent with husband Gary and in her home. Her next personal ambition is to have a family, hopefully while continuing to juggle her career!

Here is Martina's advice for the reader.

'DO . . .
- Look for variety and challenge in your work.
- Believe in yourself and your own personal and professional integrity.
- Have confidence and even if you don't, try and sound as if you have.
- Try and do everything to the best of your ability but be prepared to accept every now and again that to get the job done one has to be pragmatic.
- Look for a role model or mentor in your organisation to help lead you through the career path.
- Speak up for yourself as strongly as you feel you need to.
- Treat people fairly (even if toughly), and as you would like to be treated yourself.

DON'T . . .
- Flap.
- Criticise unnecessarily. Try and look for positive aspects.
- Take a negative attitude; try and be positive.

- Let work get out of proportion; remember that your home, family and health are what keep your sane.'

The next case history comes from Jeff Meyers of BT. He is outspoken and direct. On the matter of detail, Jeff sent in his story, which had been requested – but he added that important 'little bit extra!' He sent it on paper (hard copy) and also on disc – but the 'little bit extra' was that the disc was on the right system for the computer being used! His copy could immediately fit into the rest of the copy being prepared for this book! That is the type of attention to detail which takes a person far on his or her way to the top ...

Jeff Meyers is thirty-six and has been working at BT for twenty years. He comments:

'I come from a working class family with a younger brother and sister, Mum never worked, except at home! And Dad was a long-term (twenty-two years) officer in the Royal Navy.

'Education was varied but good, all my early education being at forces schools in Malta and Hong Kong. Later education was at a technical secondary school for boys where I stayed until completing my O levels.

'Education and life in general took a dive when first my mother became very ill, followed soon after by my father. Mum died when I was sixteen from viral meningitis (she was thirty-five). Dad died two years later from cancer; not a great start.

'School was over. I needed to earn a living and support myself.

Jobs

'I joined BT in 1971 as an engineering apprentice. Up until then I had worked off and on (mainly Saturdays) at a wet fish shop for the princely reward of £1 a day, not much money but one hell of an education – dealing with the general public, fussy/demanding housewives, handling money (including the transition to decimalisation) and keeping everybody happy. This experience would set me up well for dealing with people later.

'I loved working there, but the lure of £11 per week was too much – so I joined BT (the Post Office then)!

'**Rule**: Only take a job or move if there is something in it for you.

'Mine wasn't a great reason for choosing a job (not a career yet, you understand) but it was a start.

'For a few years I progressed within BT at a pace dictated by them (my managers). I was told – "Work hard and pass your exams (City & Guilds), and you may eventually become a Technical Officer". Not bad I thought. These TOs (technical officers) were all about twenty-five to thirty and earned a good wage, so I'll just have to bide my time.

'**Mistake**: Never be complacent.

'I got bored. My boss was an idiot and I could easily do his job, how could I sort this out?

'**Discovery**: I could dictate what I wanted to do if I put my mind to it.

'This was the starting point for getting on. All that was needed was a strategy (I didn't know it was called that then) and an action plan.

'I currently hold a middle management position in BT working as a product manager on, arguably, the largest product in the company.

'I am responsible for setting standards for customer quality and business costs for the operational parts of the business. Responsibility for quality and cost means responsibility for customer satisfaction (which means market share).

'It's all about company profitability and putting customers first, just like the fish shop but with much bigger numbers.

'They hinted that I could expect two promotions. So far I make it I've had five, one of them being the big leap from technician to manager.

Strategy

'I set my own targets for where I wanted to be, what I wanted to do, when I wanted to be there.

'I knew *why* I wanted to be there.

'I chose the right method to get there (tactics).

Advice on tactics

1 'Learn the "system"'

'You must understand the rules. For instance, if the job you are seeking requires you to dress smartly, do so while you are planning on how to get there.

'There are basic rules in all big companies. Some won't look at you for promotion until you reach certain ages or levels of education: can you fit in with this? (If not then move on.)

'My handy hints:

- you don't get promoted just by doing a good job; that's what you get paid for;
- like (generally) promotes like, e.g. if your boss is an introvert he may not be comfortable with you if you are an extrovert;
- make your face fit (even if it hurts);
- never rock the boat.

2 'Only pick winners'

'Whatever job you are currently doing, pick out at least one "project" that you know you can achieve an outstanding result on.

'Similarly, do your best to get rid of jobs that would be difficult for you. This is not as devious or bad as it may first appear. After all, as a manager you would be expected to move work to those people that were best suited to deliver for you.

'My handy hints:

- pick a job and get a result that makes your boss look good;
- deliver the result at the right time, i.e. hold back on the results if it means that you can deliver them at a key time for you, like annual appraisal or salary review time.

3 'Use people to help you progress'

'Get to know key people and be useful to them – you may be asking them for a job at some time.

'Always respect people publicly. Bad-mouthing a colleague is not a good investment, even if you have a point.

'Always listen to what people have to say.

'Always remember, it's easier to get on if your boss wants you to get on.

'My handy hints:

- don't work for the wrong boss;
- you can't do enough for a good boss.

4 'Make sure you give value for money'

'Don't spend all your time wheeling and dealing to get to your next career milestone. Remember you still have a job to do and you must be seen to do it well.

'My handy hints:

- occasionally do something for free: a bit of work that was not expected; something over a weekend for Monday morning; one of your boss's tasks that he is late on;
- don't go to the boss with problems, go with solutions;
- be professional.

5 'Make sure everyone knows it's you'

'If you do a good job, get maximum publicity. When you are low down in an organisation get yourself known for anything you can, e.g. run the sports club, arrange the Christmas lunch.

'My handy hints:

- look good: power-dress;
  be confident;
  there is no such thing as bad publicity.

6 'Use and develop all your skill areas'

'Decide what you are good at and do it, decide what you need to be good at and learn it.

'My handy hints:

- move jobs (or departments) at least every two years;
- make sure that you are at the right place at the right time, don't leave it to luck.

Steps on the way

'So far, in my career with BT I have been:

apprentice – cabinet-maker – test equipment engineer – service engineer – inspector – product auditor – process auditor – quality manager – team manager – quality consultant – project manager – product manager.

'My next moves, and my plan to get there, are secrets. I could tell you, but then I may have to kill you! (Joke!)

Imperatives

'Know what you want, make sure you know why you want it, go for it.
   'Don't rely on others, don't be complacent.
   'Understand people, fit in with them.
   'Be confident and be nice.'

And, finally, here is an unusual and intriguing case history – from Japan. In this story a young Japanese boy who had a hard early life is now one of the Japanese senate's most respected younger members of their upper house of parliament. From a childhood spent in countries such as Brazil, where at the tender age of fourteen he picked cotton and cut peanuts, he had his own 'vision'. His vision was to contribute to the world in a positive way – to help those less fortunate than himself (though at the time this seemed a wry thought). But, with ruthless honesty, he recognised that, although he had set his sights on a political career, this would take a lot to achieve, starting from where he was starting, even though he had the benefit of a caring mother and came from a political family. His father had died when he was very young, and times for the family were far from easy. So, he added up his assets, attributes and liabilities in the personal sense, and came to the conclusion that what he did have to offer was a talent for wrestling (Western style, not Sumo). Using this talent, over a relatively few years he became a champion and internationally famous. And, during this time he honed up his communication skills, and his political awareness. In doing this he came to recognise that he possessed important qualities of leadership and a certain charisma which meant that people trusted him, liked to be with him, were confident they were in safe hands, and shared his views and opinions. And so he started serious work on his lifetime ambition – to become a Japanese senator. This he achieved a few years ago.

   Today, **Senator Antonio Inoki** has a large and growing following in Japan. He speaks for the ordinary people in the world's most successful industrial country. He stands for helping the poor, helping the environment, sharing the opportunities and problems of the world. And the people love him for it. Wherever he goes there is warmth, recognition, support. Treading such a path in the Japan of today is not easy. There society is confused and there are difficulties emerging between the generations. But Antonio Inoki proceeds with enthusiasm to sell himself, his vision, his aim to make Japan a better and more kindly country. For example, single-handed he decided to travel to Iraq during the recent Gulf War, to help to free the Japanese hostages. They were duly freed! His view is that everything is possible, but you have to be honest with yourself and determined in your endeavour.

Confidence – he has plenty. But it is backed up with an innate modesty. Standing very tall, and powerful with it, Antonio Inoki has a major asset – his physical presence is unforgettable. He is Japan's 'gentle green giant', evidence that strength of purpose, hard work and good planning can reward the individual who sets out to sell him or herself towards truly worthwhile goals.

Is It Worth It?

This is the question everyone wants to have answered. Is the sacrifice, the effort, the time, the money, the frustration, the worry worth the satisfaction of finally climbing to the top of your particular mountain?

In a word, 'Yes', of course it is.

Human beings all have urge, motivation and curiosity. They want to strive to achieve something which at the present time seems beyond them, beyond their capability, beyond their reach. Ask the man who first climbed the mountain, 'Why did you do it?' and the answer is, inevitably, 'Because it is there'. Looking back through the ages, the experience of evolution and development points to the need that everyone has to develop themselves, to strive to achieve what they believe to be important.

> Great things are done when men and mountains meet:
> This is not done by jostling in the street.
>
> *William Blake*

This quotation raises an important point. You need to look from above, properly, to assess every situation.

Sometimes the sacrifices which need to be made are painful. They can lead to break up of homes, to unhappiness, to loneliness. But how much more will be the success if the sacrifices develop the family instead. If the achievement is worth while it will inevitably call for sacrifice of one sort or another. But one has only to look at the towering achievements of, say, Shakespeare, Michelangelo, Mozart, Frank Whittle (the man who invented the jet engine) and Frank Lloyd Wright (the famous architect) to see how poor the world would be without the contributions of their effort, their genius, their achievements. And they paid the price and were happy to do so, in the interests of their own fulfilment and satisfaction, and to leave the world enriched by their passage through it.

So, climbing your particular mountain is very worthwhile. Get to it. And remember, as you suffer along the way, that you are not alone. In the words of Jilly Cooper, 'You may lose on other things in life, i.e. you may find you've got to the top and not had time for your family or the people you love. Life may become a bit empty, although I don't think it happened in my case.'

The fundamental answer to the question, put to all those who helped with this book is a resounding, 'Yes, climbing to the top is very worthwhile – and it is important too that people do develop to the fullness of their potential, in the interests of us all.'

I will leave you with a comment from my husband, **Brian Locke, a chemical engineer**:

An important thought at every stage of development (of processes, machinery, systems – and people) is 'Why bother?' The answer should always be 'Because this way ahead is better than doing nothing, and leaving progress to chance'. And after each stage of development one should ask, 'Was the effort worth it, what lessons have been learnt and what does that suggest for the next stage?'

And, at the end of life, what is the answer to 'Could I bear now, not to have tried then?'

PART THREE

▲

Further Help

APPENDIX 1

────────▲────────

An ABC of Getting to the Top
Some Factors and Qualities Affecting Your Chances

A

Agenda   Where you want to end up, where others want to end up. But look out for the 'hidden' agendas; the objectives others have but don't reveal. And if you, too, have a hidden agenda, be aware of it.

Aggression   The emotional reaction of those striving hard to get their own way which reveals itself in anger and sometimes in brutal behaviour of one sort or another.

Ambition   You need to have ambition, to achieve whatever it is that you wish to achieve – it doesn't mean that you *must* become a millionaire or a chief executive.

Assertiveness   You need a good dash of assertiveness.

B

Balance   You need to be balanced, in your views, in your attitudes, in your decision-making.

Buck   Try not to 'pass the buck'. It is a practice rarely unobserved and generally despised.

C

Charisma   This doesn't half help! You either have it, or you don't. If you try to acquire it, be very careful . . . studied charisma can spell disaster.

Commitment You must have commitment if you want to be successful.

Communicating Something we are all doing all the time. Be aware of it, and recognise how good, or how bad, you are at it.

Competence In today's world of business and the professions competence matters hugely.

Complacent This means believing that things will happen whether or not you 'give them a push'. Be wary of any chance you may have of becoming complacent!

D

Determination You shouldn't fall at the first hurdle. If at first you don't succeed ... All this adds up to determination.

Discrimination A word now given to laws relating to sex and other matters. Be aware of whether or not you tend to discriminate against others and/or they against you. Consider your options on possible action most carefully.

Drive Drive is important, it is a quality sought by those recruiting for jobs.

E

Effectiveness It is very important to be effective in all you do, if possible.

Effort You should make your effort visible, but don't go overboard!

Enjoy It is most important to enjoy yourself at work. Then, and only then, can you give of your best. With only rare exceptions, this is true.

Enthusiasm A very useful attribute. People respond to enthusiasm.

Ethics To 'know yourself' you must address the subject of ethics. It is essential to know where you stand on moral questions, and your own standards of conduct and behaviour.

F

Fear Fear is a normal, human quality. If you experience it, admit it and try to do something positive about it.

Fitting in   To do well in your working life you should be sure that you are 'fitting in' − with the organisation, with your colleagues. If the 'fit' isn't right you should take this very seriously and do something about it. Either you must change or you should consider changing your job.

Flair   If you have flair you are lucky indeed!

Fun   Work should be fun!

G

General knowledge   Like common sense, it's often taken for granted. A useful attribute, but frequently not used to its best effect!

H

Hard work   Work can be hard, and hard work! Recognise this, but don't let it get the better of you.

High flyer   We all like to think of ourselves as 'high flyers'. It is important to be honest and recognise whether you are or are not a 'high flyer' in the perception of others.

Humour   A sometimes rare quality. Very valuable if used properly.

I

Image   An overworked word. Essential in today's business and professional world. Who was it said, 'A picture is worth 1,000 words . . .'? Work on your image and ensure that it is positive and not negative.

Imagination   Often overlooked. A very valuable quality if you have it. You need to know how to use it.

Integrity   Your integrity is a badge you should wear on your sleeve, visible to all, and at all times.

Intuition   One of the rare jewels in an individual's armoury. Polish it up if you have it. Use it wisely.

J

Jealousy   Sad but true. You will probably discover − and may suffer from − elements of professional jealousy from time to time. Recognise it, and try to rise above it.

Job Do it 10 per cent better than expected and the chances are you will be noticed and on your way to the top.

K

Kitchen cabinet Senior politicians have them and find them useful, so you should examine whether or not they could be useful to you. Be wary, though, they can be tricky and difficult to control.
Know-how A practical and most useful attribute.
Knowledge It should lead to wisdom. And is most valuable. Keep growing your knowledge in as many appropriate fields as possible.

L

Lateral thinking The ability to think 'sideways', usually, bringing new concepts into the issue. A most valuable attribute. It is generally present or missing, and is difficult to learn.
Listening An obvious but neglected aspect of most people's lives – business, professional or private! A pity! It can be invaluable.
Luck We all have it in some measure. Goodness knows we all need it! Recognising when we have it and when we don't is never easy but you should work at it . . .

M

Maverick Someone difficult to put a 'label' on – often tempestuous, energetic, innovative and difficult to control. Very often they have most useful contributions to make. Are you a 'maverick'? Recognise it if you are.
Mentor An experienced and trusted adviser. Find a suitable one and you will be lucky indeed.
Minor factors The small details which sometimes get to upset the applecart by confusing the entire picture! To be approached with caution . . .
Missionary zeal The total commitment which many bring to their work or the particular cause they espouse.

N

Negativeness   If you are a negative person, recognise it. And try to do something about it if you can.

Networking   Very much the trend of the 1990s – the ability to work through informal linking of like-minded people dedicated to particular subjects, areas or causes.

O

Odd one out   The square peg in the round hole. Are you one? Recognise it if you are.

Opportunity   Opportunities are generally available much more than they are recognised! Try looking out for them. They are very useful. Grab them.

Optimism   An important quality. People respond to it. But be careful to be realistic about it!

P

Persistence   This is important – but be careful not to over-egg the pudding! Don't stretch it to obstinacy . . .

Perspective   An important quality, sometimes rare. Critical to mature judgement and good, effective decision-making.

Praise   You know you like receiving it, but are you as aware as you should be of the need to give it? Be generous with praise. It is important.

Q

Qualifications   They are very important. Do get those you need to achieve your own objectives.

Quality   A much used and abused word. Try to ensure that everything you do reflects the standards of quality you have set for yourself.

R

Resources   Very necessary. Often hard to find when you need time. Ensure they are adequate for the task in hand.

Response All communications – in any form – need to evoke response. To be successful you need to be sure about the response you are seeking, and then tailor your presentations and messages to get this.

Responsibility While you may be very aware of your responsibilities to those to whom you report, are you as aware as you should be of your responsibilities to those below you on the ladder?

S

Scepticism A very useful quality. Apply healthy scepticism where you can but don't let it cloud your judgement.

Strategy Remember the importance of determining your own strategy for success.

Stress We all suffer from this – to a major or minor degree. Ensure you know the levels of stress you can take and try not to exceed them.

Sympathy An important quality – and often forgotten. We all need sympathy from time to time. Don't be one of those who doesn't notice when it is needed and is mean with giving it.

T

Thank you Remember the importance of these two little words and use them frequently, as appropriate.

Time It is very important, very expensive and can't be replaced. Try not to waste it, and learn how to manage it.

Training An essential part of today's world. Ensure you have the necessary training to equip you for the jobs and tasks you wish or need to undertake.

Trumpet Remember that it is, on occasion, important to blow your own trumpet.

Trust It is important to earn it, to keep it, and to give it.

U

Undersell Be aware if you have a tendency to undersell yourself. Correct it – but be careful how you do this.

Urbanity A confusing quality in some people. It can be useful, but it can mask a dangerous hypocrisy in some individuals. Treat it with care.

V

Vamp (Mata Hari was the original vamp). A dangerous technique some still use in trying to get to the top. Don't do it!
Vanity A dangerous affliction of some who try to get to the top – try to avoid it.

W

Work ethic Something we hear that we have forgotten! A quality still sought by employers, large and small, in those they wish to join them in enterprise. If you have it do make it known.
Worry Use it a little when creating new concepts – otherwise avoid it.

X

Xerxes Persian general whose enormous achievements were brought to nought by strategic mistakes at Thermopylae and Salamis – learn from his experience!

Y

Yes-Wo/men Beware of letting too many of them surround you – many leaders failed to stay at the top because of this temptation to which they succumbed!

Z

Zeal Useful in underlings though dangerous in excess, as it unbalances judgement.
Zeno A teacher of Socrates, who used the 'Achilles and the tortoise' story to show the absurdity of short-sighted false logic – worth bearing in mind.
Zilch For the time you spend in self-pity – this is good advice, remember it!

APPENDIX 2

─────▲─────

The Types You Might Meet on Your Way to The Top

Are you one of these types?

The Whiz Kid   He or she is on the way to the top, preferably in the fast lane. Almost always capable and competent. Often arrogant. Often with charisma. Sometimes deadly dull. Doesn't suffer fools gladly.

The Butterfly   He or she is almost always imaginative and creative. A starter but rarely a runner. They tend to 'move through' areas of work looking for the next challenge or opportunity.

The 'Gold Bricks' Merchant   He or she is solid, cautious, 'sells' the organisation line all the time, inside and outside work. Rarely creative, but oh so dependable.

The Piranha   He or she picks up other people's ideas and concepts, and makes them their own. Often aggressive, obvious, rarely with charm. Sometimes unpopular, but can be considered valuable by their bosses.

The Chameleon   He or she does not have a mind of their own. 'That's my view, if you don't like it I'll change it' is their attitude. Can be popular. Can be tricky, two-faced and dangerous.

The 'Favourite'   He or she is always trying to curry favour. With the bosses usually, but frequently at all levels. Obsequious and lacking imagination, they frequently can't see the damage they do their own chances by their attitudes and actions.

The Status Seeker   He or she is very obvious. They will do almost anything to achieve status and promotion. Sometimes they have ability. They are often aggressive.

The 'Mentor'   He or she can come in many guises. They can be very useful in spotting talent and trying to help others develop their abilities. Sometimes they go over the top in this regard, seeing themselves as more of a 'Svengali'. They are generally very valuable members of any team.

The Worthy 'Old Faithful'   He or she is a most useful and often undervalued member of the organisation. They are often 'made of twenty-four carat gold'. They can be relied on to deliver – no matter how difficult the task, or how tricky the situation. They are prepared to devote endless hours of their own time to the 'cause'. They should be given more priority in the scheme of things, but their natural modesty prevents them from pushing themselves forward. They often form the bedrock of personal added-value in the organisation.

The Corporate Bore   He or she is always predictable to say the least. They are the 'know it alls'. Whatever the question, they know the answer. Even if they don't, they pretend they do. Frequently they lack a sense of humour and a distinctive personality. On informal occasions you will find them joining groups. Groups rarely congregate around them.

The Odd One Out   He or she has a reputation for being 'an awkward beggar'. In discussion they present the opposite view, the difficult question. Frequently they have imagination, creative ability and vision. Handling them to best effect has given many a personnel director big problems.

APPENDIX 3

————▲————

Your Education and Training Matrix

In order to help you make progress along your path to the top, you should take a look at how your skills and abilities stand up to scrutiny. This example of an education and training matrix could be of help to you. It examines how someone with a potential career in the independent financial advice sector could be looked at by a potential employer.

Examine this form, and try to translate it to fit the type of job or work in which you are interested. A little time and effort spent on creating your own version of the form for your own use should prove well worthwhile.

INDEPENDENT FINANCIAL ADVICE EDUCATION AND TRAINING MATRIX

Purpose of the matrix
To set out the knowledge and skills necessary for an independent financial adviser.

This is designed as a basis for:

  i) self-assessment of training needs and career development;
 ii) appraisal of employees' skills and their development;
iii) valuation of training and education course suitability.

The matrix
The matrix is in three categories:

A knowledge;
B skills and activities;
C business skills.

Five stages of knowledge, skills or experience have been identified:

Stage 1   pre-entry requirements – basic skills and knowledge necessary for any wishing to pursue a career as an IFA – these may be obtained while working as a trainee.

Stage 2   professional starter – specific knowledge and skills essential for those broadening their career.

Stages 3 and 4   developing and operating professional – development, knowledge and skills, necessarily gained over a period of time, to become a fully rounded and experienced IFA.

Stage 5   experienced professional specialist and management – the continuing development phase from a functional to a managerial role.

IFA EDUCATION AND TRAINING MATRIX

A. **Knowledge**	Stage 1 2 3 4 5
1.	The structure of the financial services sector
2.	An appreciation of different kinds of trading concerns, as well as the legal legislative and regulatory framework of Britain and the EEC
3.	The reasons for the Financial Services Act 1986 and its effects
4.	The factors which must be present in a valid contract
5.	The nature and use of fact-find forms

Stage 1 2 3 4 5

6. The impact of different taxes on the
   financial planning process

7. National insurance contributions and
   the impact of the various social
   security benefits on financial planning

8. Investment products available in the
   market and how to make product and
   company comparisons

9. An appreciation of how pensions may
   be provided (including provision by the
   state) and the characteristics of
   pension-related benefits and AVCs

   An understanding of the ways in
   which mortgages and loans are secured

10. An appreciation of special activities
    including:
    discretionary portfolio management;

    acting as a broker fund adviser;

    acting as plan manager of a personal
    equity plan;

    acting as a scheme manager of a BES
    scheme;

    corporate finance;

    stabilising transactions;

    investments not readily realisable;

    options, warrants and other specialist
    transactions;

Stage 1 2 3 4 5

providing confirmation of investment
performance;

establishing, operating or winding up
collective investment schemes which
are not authorised unit trust schemes.

B. Skills and Activities

1. Investment planning including use of
   fact find

2. Formulating and implementing
   objectives including the use of cold
   calling and advertising

3. Identifying needs and creating demands

4. Presentation:
   advice;

   products and comparison;

   counselling and advisory techniques.

5. Identifying trends, risks and issues
   relating to investors

6. Assessing the implications for investors
   of:
   local and government dictum;

   EEC proposals and directives;

   special interest groups.

C.   Business Skills

Stage 3 4 5

Communication:

Telephone technique — All stages

Presentation technique — All stages at
personal level, stages 3, 4, 5 at executive
level

Working as part of a team — All stages at
personal level, stages 2, 3, 4, 5 need more
emphasis on this as a priority

Working as part of an organisation — All
stages at personal level, stages 3, 4, 5 will
demand more time spent in this area

Networking (clients, colleagues, contacts)

Motivation and leadership — Stages 4 and
5 will demand more emphasis on this

Induction and orientation — Stages 4 and
5 will demand priority

Interviewing and staff selection — Here
again, stages 4 and 5 will give this
priority

Organisational:

Work flow planning and setting priorities

Time management

Delegation and supervision

Budget setting and control

Team building and management

Professional development of subordinate	Stage 3 4 5
Design of financial controls	
Design of quality controls	

Analytical:

Analysing annual reports and financial data	

APPENDIX 4

————▲————

Your Competence

How competent are you? This is an important question to ask yourself. Using the checklist below will help you to examine the subject of competence, and the level at which you are happy to say that you are competent.

Are you competent at planning?

Have you prepared a presentation or proposal on planning?
Do you know how to prepare one?
Have you ever been praised or criticised about your planning abilities?
Have you recognised the need to study planning skills?

Are you competent at organising?

Have you had to organise a major event?
Have you had to organise a presentation, a debate, a conference?
Have you ever been praised or criticised about your organisational abilities?
Have you recognised the need to study organisational skills?

Are you competent at controlling?

Have you had to control people? Budgets? Work schedules? The purchase of equipment? Services?
Have you studied the control of people or projects?

Have you ever been praised or criticised about your ability to control processes, activities or people?

Are you competent at development?

Have you been in charge of a development project?
Have you worked on a development project?
Are you familiar with the methodology of development projects?
Have you recognised the need to study development processes?

Are you competent at interaction?

Have you ever led a team?
Have you experience of giving directions and seeing your instructions carried out?
Are you familiar with the differing aspects of roles, duties, procedures etc. to maximise the performance of teams?
Have you considered what is required in all the many components that make up effective interaction?
Have you recognised the need to develop the skills needed for effective interaction?

Having gone through this checklist, you should have an idea of your level of competence. You can decide what needs to be done. Now let us look at some other aspects of competence.

Are you efficiency-oriented?

If you strive to improve what you are doing, to do it better, and to focus on the degree of progress you are making against a standard of excellence, then the answer must be 'Yes'. If not, then you should examine what needs to be done and whether or not you should set about doing it.

Are you proactive?

If you initiate activities, proposals or communications to accomplish a project or a task, rather than to wait to react to a problem emerging, then the answer must be 'Yes'. If not, you should either accept this, recognising that it may inhibit your progress to the top, or take action to correct your attitude and reactions.

Are you good at diagnosis?

If you seek to examine different concepts to gather information about the task you have in hand, and can then decide what the situation (problem, opportunity or potential for development) offers and needs, then the answer must be 'Yes'. If not, you should examine the overall issue and decide what action to take.

Are you good at persuasion?

If you are concerned with power, reputation and the objects and behaviour associated with status, it follows that you should be good at persuading others to your point of view. Are you?

Are you self-confident?

If you believe in what you are doing, and in your success; if you are forceful, and express little ambivalence at taking a decision, then the answer must be 'Yes'. Whatever you lack, you should work to fill the gaps.

Are you objective?

If you view the task from a multiple perspective − taking in the customer's point of view, as well as the managers' and the shareholders' points of view, also the different relationships involved, and looking at the pros and cons of each in arriving at a decision, then the answer must be 'Yes'. Do not deny emotion, or forget the importance of urge (vision, capability and determination), and of what you want to achieve − but you must be able to see situations objectively.

APPENDIX 5

▲

Your CV

Your CV is unquestionably an important document. How you present yourself to a potential employer, or for an important assignment or project which you wish to undertake, is critical to your chances of success. So how should you go about it? Remember the overall pupose of a CV – whether you are responding to an advertisement or writing in cold – is to secure an interview.

The first thing to recognise is the fact that a CV can be written in many ways. You can write your CV so that it is a dry, dusty record of what happened to you in the chronological sense, starting at the beginning with your education and ending up with details of the most recent job you have performed. Or you can write your CV so that it gives the reader more of a 'flavour' of the type of person you are, what you have achieved, what you are most interested in achieving. In other words you can make your CV spell out the extra qualities which you can bring to the job, given the chance.

A compromise is to write your CV so that it is factual and highlights your accomplishments and abilities, putting your selling points for the job up front and spelling them out.

The choice as to which approach you should take is up to you. You can get help from many of the recruitment consultants who advertise regularly in the general and specialist press. They will make a charge, but many people have benefitted as a result. So consider this option.

If you want to proceed under your own steam, pause again

for thought. If you prepare your CV in general terms, you should then take the trouble to create a specific version for the job application you have in mind. Making this extra effort can be very worthwhile. It spells out to the reader that you have thought about the matter from his/her point of view. And it can unquestionably save his/her time, which is an extra courtesy you have extended in recognition of the pressures at the reader's end. Such consideration shown by a would-be employee will, generally, count in their favour.

Once you have decided on the content of your CV, you must next consider its presentation. Here are some tips which should be useful:

- DO ensure immaculate presentation of your CV. Check that the spelling is accurate, the typing is excellent and professional, and that it is reproduced on good quality paper.

- DO send out the CV – and supporting letter – so that it remains pristine until the envelope is opened. Never fold it. Ensure that the envelope, too, looks good and is accurately addressed, preferably to the person by name, with the correct spelling, job title, etc.

- DON'T write a book – ensure that the CV fits on one or two pages at most.

- DO list business-related activities (organisations you are a member of, any awards you may have received), not personal activities unless relevant to the job or its circumstances. And add whether or not you drive and have a car and a clean driving licence.

- DON'T include information on what salary you received in your last job, or what salary you are looking for – this information will be called for when you have secured an interview.

- DO send a covering letter with your CV. Make it short, friendly and courteous.

- DO CHECK AND DOUBLE CHECK – preferably asking someone to help you – to ensure that there are no inaccuracies or slips in terms of spelling or presentation. Your CV must make maximum impact on the person reviewing it, and stand out from the others. A small slip up can cost you the chance of the interview!

So what should your CV look like? Here is an example of a general purpose CV for you to work on. Use it to produce your own version.

CURRICULUM VITAE

JACK SMITH
20 Clarebury Gardens
Glastonbury Street
London
SW4 8QJ

Telephone: 071–694 1512

British Born: 23 February 1953 Married with two children

Experienced ACCOUNT DIRECTOR with expertise in developing UK and European marketing strategies, translating them into marketing and sales programmes to agreed objectives, and meeting the targets set. Significant efficiencies and strong sales successes have been achieved. Flair for creative thinking, organising and negotiating. Adaptable, level headed and strong team leader.

Voluntarily leaving existing post in June 1992 as company relocating to Frankfurt.

CAREER BACKGROUND

1985–1992 **ACCOUNT DIRECTOR**
The ABC International Advertising Group
Responsibility for leading account teams operating UK and European programmes on behalf of the following brand leading companies:

X, Y, Z

Responsibility for working with clients at director and senior management level for advertising budget expenditures totalling £7m annually.

1976–1985 **MARKETING MANAGER**
EFG PLC (Consumer Goods Division)

Responsible to Marketing Director for marketing and sales programmes in support of twelve branded products, selling through UK supermarkets. Total sales approximately £50m annually. Responsibilities included selection and briefing of advertising agencies and other outside suppliers, liaison with these organisations and setting of projected budgets for brands, evaluation of operations of campaigns against targets, and presentations to sales teams and other company reporting structures. Responsibilities also included external liaison with specialist press and relevant media, also selected opinion formers and trade bodies.

1974–1976 **TRAINEE ACCOUNT EXECUTIVE**
KLM Advertising

Work in Creative, Copywriting, Media and Print Buying Departments, followed by work in account teams and 3 months as PA to Board Director. Special permission given to allow research work on behalf of Conservative Member of Parliament, Mr X MP.

BACKGROUND AND QUALIFICATIONS

Education: Bradfield, Reading, 7 'O' Levels, 3 'A' Levels, 2 'S' Levels
Exeter University, BA (Hons) Politics and Economics

Memberships: Publicity Club of London
                     Marketing Society
                     Chartered Institute of Marketing
                     Institute of Directors

Car owner, clean driving licence

Finally, in developing your CV, always bear in mind the main information which must be transferred to the reader:

- Your objective
- Your abilities
- Your major accomplishments
- Your work history
- That important and 'special' extra dimension you will bring to the other party – given the chance!

APPENDIX 6

▲

Your Appraisal Form

In today's world of business the annual appraisal is an important occasion, both for you and your employer. It is becoming increasingly popular to use a specially prepared form for this purpose, and to arrange for it to be filled out by the employee. You are thus in a position to assist in your own appraisal. The selected official of the firm will discuss with you how he or she agrees or disagrees with what is written on the form. And finally you will both 'sign the form off' having reached a consensus.

This form of 'open' appraisal is, indeed, enlightened. It enables an honest transfer of views between the two people involved, and there is no hint of decisions being taken 'behind closed doors'.

The form on page 210 is an example of the type of appraisal form used by major organisations. This is based on a job in a major financial institution, to fit in with the other appendices in this book.

APPRAISAL FORM

Appointed Officers
Annual Report for Period _____ to _____ 19 _____

Surname: _____ Forenames: _____
Mr/Mrs/Miss/Ms   Marital status:

Branch/Dept: _____ Salary: _____

Job title: _____ Grade: _____ Tier: _____

Date of birth:_____ Date of entry:_____ Date joined grade:_____

Date joined present Branch/Dept: _____

Address: _____

Telephone: _____ Date of occupation:_____

Tenure: Owner occupier/Bank owned/Rented/Lodgings/With parents

Dependent children

M/F _____ Date of birth _____

M/F _____ Date of birth _____

Qualification   Prt.1/Stg.1   Prt.2/Stg.2   Stg.3
                                           BKG T'tee Int FSD

Institute of Bankers Diploma Examinations

If completed specify dates passed:

If not completed specify subjects passed:

State prizes, distinctions, if any:

Is the intention to complete?   Stage 2:   Stage 3:

Highest educational level completed: CSE   O   A   Univ   Other

Qualifications other than IOB held:

being pursued:

Languages (inc Welsh) in which you are fluent:

Car/motor cycle driver: Yes/No

Own transport available for travel to and from work: Yes/No

Outside interests/Clubs/Societies:

Experience during last ten years, starting with present position

Branch/Dept _____ No of Staff ____

Position/Duties _____

Grade _____ Period Year/Months _____

Internal courses and attachments attended (state year):

External courses attended (State year):

Branch/Dept _____ No of Staff ____

Position/Duties _____

Grade _____ Period Year/Months _____

Internal courses and attachments attended (state year):

External courses attended (State year):

Branch/Dept _____ No of Staff ____

Position/Duties _____

Grade _____ Period Year/Months _____

Internal courses and attachments attended (state year):

External courses attended (State year):

Interest expressed in following Departments/Divisions:

Next of kin (Name):
(Person to be contacted in case of need)

Address:

Telephone:

Part 1: Performance – Appointed Officers

Name of member of staff:

Branch/Department: _____ Period ____ to ____ 19 ____

Lowest score indicator   1 2 3 4 5 6   *Highest score indicator*

Motivation

Slow and undisciplined in the approach to specific tasks, thus setting a poor example to subordinates.

1 2 3 4 5 6

Consistently energetic, confident and disciplined in the approach to tasks. Successfully encourages a similar approach by subordinates.

Self-appraisal mark   ☐

Technical competence

Has difficulty in acquiring appropriate technical knowledge and skills and generally requires assistance to revolve technical problems.

1 2 3 4 5 6

Consistently able to acquire and apply appropriate technical knowledge to the effective solution of customer/office needs and problems with little or no assistance.

Self-appraisal mark   ☐

Setting and meeting priorities

Fails to allocate own or subordinates time effectively with the result that work is disorganised, objectives unmet and time wasted. Usually seeks assistance in dealing with barriers.

1 2 3 4 5 6

Consistently demonstrates an ability to establish priorities accurately, to manage time effectively and to respond appropriately to barriers. Ensures that subordinates achieve deadlines and meet objectives.

Self-appraisal mark   ☐

Customer orientation

Does not understand the need to give customer service priority, does not structure own work or that of others to meet customer needs, takes little part in activities designed to improve the quality of service, insensitive and tactless with customers and does not set appropriate standards for subordinates.

1 2 3 4 5 6

Understands need to give customer service priority, structures own work or that of others to meet customer needs, takes a full part in activities designed to improve the quality of service, deals sensitively and tactfully with customers and sets the same standards for subordinates.

Self-appraisal mark ☐

Sensitivity to staff

Insensitive and tactless, tends to say and do the wrong thing at the wrong time.

1 2 3 4 5 6

Sensitive and tactful, consistently able to use the appropriate behaviour to deal with all levels of staff.

Self-appraisal mark ☐

Decision-making

Avoids making decisions or makes poor decisions.

1 2 3 4 5 6

Consistently makes soundly-based decisions.

Self-appraisal mark ☐

Problem-solving skills

Fails to solve problems and/or is confused or muddled in approaching solutions.

1 2 3 4 5 6

Consistently produces logical and clear solutions to problems.

Self-appraisal mark ☐

Volume of work

Unable to complete the tasks allocated within an acceptable time-scale.

1 2 3 4 5 6

Consistently completes the tasks allocated well within expected time-scales.

Self-appraisal mark ☐

Team skills

Tends to work alone and generally is distanced from colleagues and subordinates. Prone to generating strain or conflict in relationships.

1 2 3 4 5 6

Fits readily into any group and demonstrates a marked facility for developing effective relationships with colleagues and subordinates.

Self-appraisal mark ☐

Leadership skills

Unable to control others, delegate work or train effectively.

1 2 3 4 5 6

An outstanding and respected leader who sets a high example. Trains effectively and delegates where appropriate.

Self-appraisal mark ☐

Accuracy

Does not complete work allocated to the level of accuracy required.

1 2 3 4 5 6

Consistently able to complete all the work allocated to the level of accuracy required.

Self-appraisal mark ☐

Reaction to change

Unadaptable and inflexible. Does not understand, accept or cope with changing circumstances.

1 2 3 4 5 6

Adaptable and flexible. Consistently able to grasp and cope effectively with changing circumstances. Successfully encourages subordinates to do the same.

Self-appraisal mark ☐

215

Communication skills, written

Writes in a confused,
illogical and imprecise
way.

1 2 3 4 5 6

Demonstrates a
consistently fluent, logical
and precise written style.

Self-appraisal mark ☐

Communication skills, oral

Speaks in a confused,
illogical and imprecise
way.

1 2 3 4 5 6

Demonstrates a
consistently fluent, logical
and precise spoken style.

Self-appraisal mark ☐

Attitude to authority

Resents authority.
Unwilling to exercise
control over others.
Cannot take a firm line
when necessary.

1 2 3 4 5 6

Consistently demonstrates
the ability to co-operate
with authority.
Successfully exercises
control over others being
fair but firm when
necessary.

Self-appraisal mark ☐

Marking key: (Circle the appropriate number each time)

1 Frequently fails to meet

2 Occasionally falls short of

3 Fully meets

4 Occasionally exceeds   the requirements of the job

5 Frequently exceeds

6 Consistently exceeds

Voluntary self-appraisal: If the member of staff so wishes, the appropriate mark 1 to 6 should be inserted in each self-appraisal box.

Part 2: Potential – Appointed Officers

Lowest score indicator   1 2 3 4 5 6   *Highest score indicator*

The need for success

Does not respond to   1 2 3 4 5 6   Shows a positive response
encouragement or criticism,   to encouragement and
avoids challenges.   criticism, seeks and
           responds well to challenges.

Self-appraisal mark   ☐

Personal qualities

Unassertive, lacking in self   1 2 3 4 5 6   Assertive, self confident
confidence and discipline.   and disciplined. Able to win
Passive, lacks   respect. Demonstrates
determination.   alertness, energy and
           determination.

Self-appraisal mark   ☐

Career attitudes

Has a negative attitude.   1 2 3 4 5 6   Always displays a positive
Unconcerned about   attitude. Has high personal
personal standards, lacks   standards, makes a positive
personal commitment to   personal contribution to all
tasks and/or career progress.   tasks and seeks additional
Lacks personal goals for   responsibility. Sets personal
advancement.   goals and seeks oppor-
           tunities for career
           progression.

Self-appraisal mark   ☐

Professional standards and qualifications

Unconcerned about   1 2 3 4 5 6   Demonstrates high
professional standards and   professional standards.
qualifications.   Shows outstanding progress
           in obtaining professional
           qualifications.

Self-appraisal mark   ☐

217

Relationships with management

| Unwilling to play a part in the management 'team'. Reluctant to approach management or does so in a diffident or disrespectful manner. Unable to anticipate needs. Is unwilling to seek information or express opinions. | 1 2 3 4 5 6 | Seeks to play an integral part in the management 'team'. Responds to management in an outgoing and questioning way. Anticipates needs. Prepared to seek information and express opinions. |

Self-appraisal mark ☐

Relationships with others (including customers where appropriate)

| Has difficulty in relating to others. Avoids involvement. | 1 2 3 4 5 6 | Relates easily and professionally to people establishing rapport in any group irrespective of its members' status. |

Self-appraisal mark ☐

Creativity

| Uses only a routine and unoriginal approach to situations and challenges. | 1 2 3 4 5 6 | Consistently demonstrates a creative, original and innovative approach to situations and challenges. |

Self-appraisal mark ☐

Outside knowledge and involvement

| Very limited knowledge or interest in broader issues. Lack of any community social or professional involvement. | 1 2 3 4 5 6 | Demonstrates extensive knowledge of and interest in broader issues. Plays a leading role in community social and/or professional activities. |

Self-appraisal mark ☐

Marking Key: (Circle the appropriate number each time)

1 **Frequently** fails to display the appropriate qualities and attitudes

2 **Occasionally** fails to display the appropriate qualities and attitudes

3 **Usually** displays the appropriate qualities and attitudes to a satisfactory level

4 **Occasionally** displays above average qualities and attitudes

5 **Frequently** displays the appropriate qualities and attitudes to a high level

6 **Consistently** displays the appropriate qualities and attitudes to a high level

Voluntary self-appraisal: If the member of staff so wishes, the appropriate mark 1 to 6 should be inserted in each self-appraisal box.

Comments Sheet

Name of member of staff:

Branch/Department: _____ Period _____ to _____ 19 _____

To be completed by the member of staff

Brief description of normal duties:

Highest grade for which qualified for deputisation purposes:

What do you see as your probable next job?

How far do you see your career developing?

Are there any factors you would like the company to bear in mind when considering transfers etc.?

219

Other comments you wish to record (including training, development, periods of responsibility etc.)

_____

To be completed by the reporting officer

(Comments should include reference to above section, any training and development aspects and, where appropriate, health/attendance, punctuality and appearance and dress)

Signature _____ Name_____

Position_____ Period of close association _____

_____

To be completed by the branch/department manager

Signature _____ Name_____

Date _____ Period of close association _____

APPENDIX 7

▲

Job Specification

When you apply for a job always bear in mind that those who are seeking to fill the post should already have a clear idea of what and who they are looking for. They will have drawn up a job specification which sets out in detail the experience, skills and other qualities being sought. You need to try to fit with their ideas.

Naturally, it is not always possible to make the most perfect fit between the applicant and the job specification. However, the specification will help those making the appointment to see what the different applicants have to offer and where the gaps lie.

So, what does a job specification look like? How detailed is it? How clearly does it set out what the organisation is seeking in the person to be appointed to the job? If you are familiar with job specifications, this should also help you to create your own CV.

Here is a specimen of a job specification for a relatively senior executive in a trade association.

JOB TITLE   SECRETARY OF THE ASSOCATION
DIRECTOR OF ADMINISTRATION

JOB PURPOSE   i) as an officer of the association to perform the duties of secretary, reporting to the chairman and council of the association

                 ii) as director of administration to ensure the proper functioning of the association including its financial affairs

221

iii) as an authorised deputy of the chief
executive act on his behalf in his absence

DIMENSIONS

People: 7 direct reporting
28 in total in three sub-units
Budget: £4 million
Authority for expenditure (sole authority)
Revenue: Within budget £
Outside budget £
Capital: Within budget £
Outside budget £

ORGANISATION CHART

SECRETARY AND DIRECTOR OF ADMINISTRATION

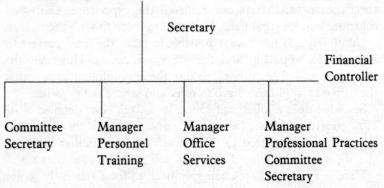

ACCOUNTABILITIES

Act as company secretary in order to discharge the duties required
by the Companies Act in arranging general and council meetings
and ensuring the proper recording of the proceedings of these
meetings and of all meetings of committees of the council.

Draft and distribute ALL communications with members on
behalf of the council of the association in order to ensure complete
consistency and clarity of transmission of council's decisions.

Direct the recruitment and maintenance of the human and
physical resources of the association (excluding computer

equipment) through managers responsible for personnel/training and office services in order to ensure that all departments are adequately serviced within budget.

Control all letters of appointment and termination of employment and consult with the trustees on pension matters in order to ensure compliance with employment legislation.

Maintain a career development programme and advise the chief executive on salary review matters in order that all members of staff are adequately trained and rewarded for the jobs that they are required to perform.

Direct the financial controller in meeting statutory financial requirements and advise the finance and general purposes committee on all financial matters, including the expected impact on members.

Negotiate insurance contracts for people, premises, other assets and professional indemnity to meet the agreed employment and other policies and statutory requirements and to keep these requirements under review.

SPECIAL FEATURES

A complete knowledge of the association constitution and its interrelation with legal and other official regulations is necessary to advise council and committees on their proper activities.

A full familiarity with the duties of director as required by the Companies Act is essential.

An unusually broad band of responsibility calls for particular tact and diplomacy in dealing with all levels of authority.

APPENDIX 8

---▲---

Action Plan for 'You' Limited

The word 'Limited' means confined between limits. In business it has a whole range of specific legal (and tax) responsibilities that apply to everyone in some way or other – including you. So the concept of 'You' Ltd needs to be qualified, because what we are talking about is the exploration of your potential. However, it is an apt analogy to consider that you, as a person, can be viewed as a 'property', with assets and liabilities, with a cost of operation, with a 'customer base', and with an existing and a potential market.

So, if you want to look at yourself this way, how do you set about it? First, you need to take a look at 'You' Ltd on a balance sheet. This is not as difficult as it sounds.

Take the annual report and accounts of the organisation you work for. Now consider yourself in a similar light. The first elements to examine are the assets and liabilities of 'You' Ltd.

Your assets

Yourself, what you are, what you know, what you promise, what you are able to deliver. The 'value for money' that you can be said to represent. The 'added-value' you bring to your employers, to those you work with, to your family and friends, as well as to your colleagues – whether you are employed by an organisation or are your own boss. These are your 'assets'.

Your liabilities

Yourself, what you don't know, the disappointment between what you promise and what you deliver. The costs of extending your knowledge, your training and competence, and of ensuring that your vision and horizons can be widened — to the benefit of your employers, your family, friends and colleagues and to yourself. These are your 'liabilities'. They include the investment (time, effort, even money), represented and necessary to take you from where you are now, to where you plan to be within given periods of time. Your liabilities can also include commitments of your time to others, and your inability to manage your time and your money to maximum effect.

Your 'profit and loss account'

On the one side you have your income and related benefits, and on the other your expenditures and commitments. Seen in the wider sense, your income can include items other than money — for example, the additions to your knowledge and experience over time, adding to your value. Your liabilities, too, can include items other than money — for example, commitments to others and the inability to find the necessary time and energy to try to extend your knowledge and to take advantage of your opportunities for education and training, or to widen your intellectual and other horizons.

Your business plan

This really should be looked at as your 'action plan'. It should include information about your 'customer base' — this could be one employer, sundry key contacts, your opportunities to 'network' to the benefit of your employers and yourself — but it may be very different according to your particular type of activity and lifestyle.

Your opportunities to plan for the future so that you can add to your value, in your working career, and in terms of citizenship, also in personal terms as a parent, a friend or a colleague, should also be spelt out, together with a note of the action needed from you, and any costs of time and expenditure involved.

Any business or action plan should allow for unexpected happenings which may throw the plan off course. These could be in terms of developments at work, in the home, or with the family.

At the end of the day you want to know where you stand now, where you would like to stand in the future and how to plan towards achieving this.

Your balance sheet

As with any balance sheet, you will need to work on the above information in order to draw some conclusions. You will need to know whether the assets outweigh the liabilities or if the balance lies the other way round. If the latter is the case, you need to accept that you need to do something to correct the position!

Your action plan

This needs to be drawn up as a series of points for action, with these points related to your resources of time and money available and/or needed.

Even if this is a touch light-hearted in terms of a concept, it should serve to focus your attention on an important area, and at least it will offer you some signposting as to how to set about drawing up your action plan for 'You' Ltd.

Look at the following example:

Joe Soap Limited

Involved in Joe Soap Limited are:

Joe Soap
Mary Soap (his wife)
Jennifer and David Soap (the children)
The ABC organisation for whom Joe works
Joe's colleagues at work
Joe's friends
The organisations of which Joe is a member
(for starters ...)

The principal activity of Joe Soap in his work as a marketing executive in the ABC organisation.

The 'share capital' of Joe Soap includes himself, his qualifications, the added-value he gives to the organisation for whom he works, the organisations of which he is a member, and the courses on which he is recruited in terms of adding to his qualifications, training and competence.

The fixed assets of Joe Soap include his experience and know-how, his share of the house, the car, the bank balance and so on.

Profit and Loss Account for Joe Soap Limited

Joe's turnover is represented by his salary and any other money, such as what he earns from, for example, freelance consultancy, investment income or the equivalent etc.

Joe's operating costs include what it costs for him and his family to live, (food, holidays, clothes, school fees, mortgage payments etc.), the costs of subscriptions, the provision for saving and investment, and so on.

The difference between what Joe receives as income (from salary, any fees, savings and investment income etc.), and what he spends, represents his 'profit'.

Balance Sheet for Joe Soap Limited

Joe's balance sheet will include his assets (as described earlier), and also his liabilities. These will include what he owes, his commitments to everyone involved, and time and other resources which he has 'mortgaged' to his future. His assets, less his liabilities will give him a true picture of where he stands today.

His next move is to prepare his action plan.

Action Plan for Joe Soap Limited

The first priority for Joe is to look at where he would like to be in a year's time from the day he completed his balance sheet. This should establish targets for progress and points for action. Progress should be looked at in terms of money (increase in proportion of savings with, hopefully, a decrease in proportion of liabilities); job progression; family progression, progression in terms of involvement in extramural activities and so on.

Then Joe should set about preparing a snapshot picture of where he would like to be in five years' time.

The use of a simple discipline such as the one outlined in this appendix should go a long way to help Joe to plan his future so that it is more rewarding to him and his family in all senses of those words.

APPENDIX 9

▲

Being Your Own Boss

It all starts with you. You must know what you have to bring to a new venture. At this time it is a decision for you alone. Having a gut feeling that you want to do it isn't enough. You must know what you will bring to any new business. The rewards of success can be great, but the costs of failure can be catastrophic.

Who can help

You will have some ideas as to why you want to start a business, and whether or not this is a new urge. You should also know, in very basic terms, whether or not there is a market for your initiative, and if you have the energy to take on the commitment to long hours and the stress that will almost inevitably be involved. So, who can help you at this stage?

Friends, relatives and colleagues can offer help and advice, but you should be careful not to overestimate what they can do, or the wishful thinking element which may be in their advice, willing you to succeed and being hesitant to point out some of the snags.

Your potential future customers for the business can also help – doing a straw poll or even some market research is very important, usually essential. You *must* establish that there *is* a market for your new enterprise before you start.

Compiling a profile of your future competitors can help – researching who is and who is not a competitor, the success they enjoy and the difficulties they encounter is important to you by way of essential background to your planning.

Your financial and legal advisers (bank, accountant, investment advisers, lawyers) can help. And they should be seen as performing a critically important role, both for the advice they can give, and for the endorsement of the seriousness and worthwhileness of your venture they can provide.

Your options

In basic terms, these are:

to operate as a sole trader;
to set up in partnership with one or more others;
to set up a limited company.

All these options need detailed prior study, as regards starting off, running the enterprises, shutting down, getting out, retiring, selling your share etc. There are, of course, pros and cons for each, and within each there can be variants. What is essential is to study the differences and to decide which is the best route for you, in being your own boss, to develop and carry on the business you want to do.

There are many types of business operation, where you can be your own boss, related to using your expertise. Some involve making, or selling, or providing services, others to franchise-type operations, for example (where you decide to buy a franchise and sell the franchise company's products or services, using its name, logo, experience, guidance and often its suppliers and materials).

A further type of business operation is the co-operative where everyone shares responsibilities for the decisions, the rewards and the problems. You could operate as an ordinary limited company or have limited liability by being registered under the Industrial and Provident Societies Act.

Whatever route you want to follow, it is essential to do your homework as, while being your own boss can be exciting and make you successful, it can also be a tempestuous sea for those who don't know – or can't find out quickly – how to swim in it!

The first steps to make progress

The first point is that you will be setting up a business – with taxes, accounts, return on capital, expenditures on labour, overheads and other direct costs. You must start with the preparation of a business plan. This is important to keep you on a straight course in relation to the development of the business. In writing a business plan you must cover the following important elements:

the definition of the business;
who will be involved and how;
the objectives;
the strategy to be used to achieve your objectives;
the plan of operation;
the financial plan;
your plan for future development.

Presenting your business plan

Having written your business plan, you must review it in relation to whom you will be presenting it. It may be that you need financial help, from other shareholders, from your bank, from your colleagues. Your accountants will be able to offer you advice on sources of finance available from government and other bodies.

Running your business

Before you start out on the road to being your own boss, there are some factors to consider in relation to running the operation when you have started it. Here is a list of things to think about.

Location Is it good – for offices, operations, storage and/or other requirements? Is there adequate access – for deliveries, dispatches, customers, car-parking, passing trade, waste disposal?

Potential Can you genuinely expect to increase turnover and profit? How much? What is the picture regarding competition? Can the product or service be improved as time goes on?

Business Is the reputation of the business likely to be good? Can it be improved? Are systems adequate and up to date? Are there good intelligence systems to ensure that you are kept up to date?

Price Is the pricing structure reasonable and competitive?

Have you the flexibility to cope with changes in demand? In competition?

Equipment and buildings   Are these adequate and do they represent value for money? What about wear and tear? Becoming out of date? Cost of replacement?

Staff   Do you have adequate staffing resources? Will staff prove helpful in the new situation? Are salaries and wages reasonable but adequate? What about sickness? Competitors subverting your staff?

Finally, is there a trade association to join? And a chamber of commerce? These types of bodies can be very helpful in a start-up situation.

Summary

- If you want to be your own boss it is important to know yourself, to know what you have to offer; and to take practical steps to examine all the key issues involved from finance to competition.

- To run your own business you must devote adequate time to planning – ensuring that your feet are kept firmly on the ground, while still being imaginative.

- Talk to the banks about their services and their information packs in relation to setting up and running small businesses.

- Recognise where the sources of help are, so that you can turn to them when you need help, advice, external expertise and, if necessary, finance.

- Finally, don't start on this path unless and until you have established that there is a genuine market out there for you to explore and to exploit.

APPENDIX 10

▲

Defining Your Position as A Communicator

You need to determine whether or not you are a good communicator. Here is a checklist which should be helpful.

- You have a message to impart. Can you write it in seventeen words? Try it and see. Can you say it in fewer? (Top specialists in communication have discovered this is the key to good communication.)

- There is a right and a wrong time to communicate. Can you tell which is which? For example, would you talk to your boss about a difficulty you are experiencing in your work at a social function of the organisation?

- When you are discussing something important, have you considered in advance the response you wish to evoke from the listener?

- When you have made an appointment to see someone to discuss an important issue, do you prepare in advance? How? By acknowledging the time-frame of the meeting? By setting out a few points (say three) that you wish to discuss? By assessing and identifying the desirable outcome you would like from the meeting?

- Have you ever examined how good you are on paper? Try giving yourself points out of ten for communcation and apply this technique also to those you know whom you consider better at this art.

● Have you ever considered whether you are good or bad at debate? On paper? Orally? Again, try marking yourself against others to find out whether you are better or worse than they are.

● Have you considered whether or not you are fluent and/or lucid as a communicator? It could be that communicating comes easily to you, or you may be one of those who have to draft, redraft and redraft again before you get a letter, a speech, an article to your satisfaction.

● Faced with an opportunity to speak up – at a small or large function, or on radio or television, is your instinctive reaction to try to duck the opportunity, or to grab it and learn from it?

● Do you recognise the need for research on issues which you believe important and on which you may wish to comment at some time? Do you keep files with snippets of key information for possible future use?

● Do you rehearse time and again before making a key speech or speaking in an important debate or committee meeting?

● Are you good or bad at those important 'one-liners' (the short, snappy comment which expresses the point succinctly)?

● Do others tend to quote your comments on big and small issues?

BIBLIOGRAPHY

Alberti, Robert E. and Emmons, Michael L. *Your Perfect Right* California: Impact Press, 1974.

Aleksander, Tobe *The Right to be Yourself* London: Piatkus Books, 1992.

Bach, George and Goldberg, Herb *Creative Aggression* New York: Doubleday, 1974.

Back, Ken and Back, Kate *Assertiveness at Work* London: MacGraw – Hill, 1982.

Barham, K. and Rassam, C. *Shaping The Corporate Future* London: Unwin Hyman Ltd, 1989.

Bernstein, D. *Put It Together, Put It Across* London: Cassell Publishers Ltd, 1988.

Bower, S. A. and Bower, G. H. *Asserting Yourself* New York: Addison-Wesley Publishing Company, 1988.

De Bono, E. *I Am Right, You Are Wrong* London: Penguin Books, 1991.

Bryce, L. *The Influential Woman* London: Piatkus Books, 1989.

Burton, A. *A Programmed Guide to Office Warfare* London: Panther Books, 1971.

Dilenschneider, R. with Beyma, R. *Power and Influence* London: Business Books Limited, 1991.

Ellis, W. D. and Siedel, F. *How To Win Conferences, Meetings And Interviews* New York: Prentice-Hall, 1955.

Goldsmith, W. and Clutterbuck, D. *The Winning Streak* London: George Weidenfeld and Nicolson Ltd, 1984.

Goyder, G. *The Responsible Worker* London: Hutchinson & Co, 1975.

Hare, Beverley *Be Assertive* London: Optima, 1988.

Jones, A. *How to Build A Successful Career* London: Business Books Ltd, 1991.

Leeds, D. *Marketing Yourself* London: Piatkus Books, 1991.

McCormick, D. *Taken For A Ride* Dorset, UK: Harwood-Smart Publishing Co. Ltd, 1976.

Pease, A. *Body Language* London: Sheldon Press, 1990.

Peters, T. J. and Waterman, R. H. Jr. *In Search of Excellence* New York: Harper and Row, 1982.

Rassam, C. *Secrets Of Success* London: Sidgwick and Jackson Ltd, 1988.

Savage, P. *Who Cares Wins* London: Mecury Books, 1987.

Schroder, Harold M. *Managerial Competence − The key to excellence* Kendall/Hunt Publishing Company, Dubuque, Iowa, USA.

Thomas, H. with Gill, L. *Making An Impact* Devon, U.K.: David and Charles, 1989.

Thornely, N. and Lees, D. *How To Be A Winner* London: Mercury, 1989.

Ward, C. *Company Courtesy* Hants: Gower Publishing Co Ltd, 1989.

Willis, L. and Daisley, J. *Springboard* Stroud, Glos: Hawthorn Press, 1990.

INDEX